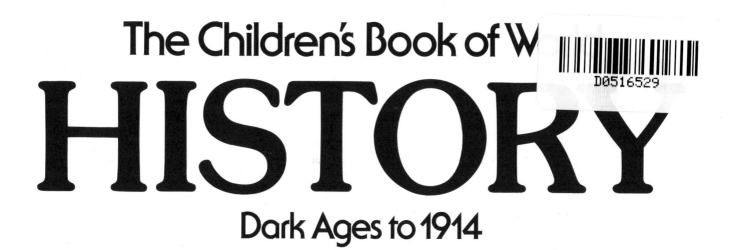

The Children's Book of World HISTORY

Dark Ages to 1914

Dr Anne Millard

Illustrated by Joseph McEwan
Designed by Graham Round
Edited by Robyn Gee and Jenny Tyler

The material in this book is also published as three separate titles in the Usborne Picture World History series: *Crusaders, Aztecs, Samurai, Exploration and Discovery* **and** *The Age of Revolutions.*

Contents

Consultant Editors: Brian Adams, Verulamium Museum, St Albans, England; D. Barrass, University of East Anglia, England; Professor Edmund Bosworth, Dept of Near Eastern Studies, University of Manchester, England; Ben Burt, Museum of Mankind, London, England; Elizabeth Carter, Institute of Archaeology, London, England; Dr M. C. Chapman, University of Hull, England; T. R. Clayton, University of Cambridge, England; Dr M. Falkus, London School of Economics, England; Professor Norman Hampson, University of York, England; George Hart, British Museum, London, England; Dr C. J. Heywood, University of London, England; Peter Johnston, Commonwealth Institute, London, England; Dr Michael Loewe, University of Cambridge, England; Dr M. McCauley, University of London, England; Dr J. A. Sharpe, University of York, England; Dr C. D. Sheldon, University of Cambridge, England; R. W. Skelton, Victoria & Albert Museum, London, England; Dr R. Waller, University of Cambridge, England.

Picture research by Penni O'Grady

About this Book

This book begins at a time when a new religion, Islam, was beginning in the Middle East. Europe was in chaos. The Romans' well-ordered government had been ended around AD400 by invading hordes of barbarians. The time that followed is often know as the European "Dark Ages".

This book describes some of the main developments in Europe from the end of the Dark Ages to the outbreak of World War I. It also tells about the civilisations of Africa, America, India and the Far East and what happened when European explorers found them.

When the barbarians invaded Europe they brought their own religions with them, but the Christians who were left tried to convert them. This picture illustrates one of the stories from this time. It tells of St Coifi, a Christian, who lived in the north of England.

He wanted to show the heathens how powerless their gods were, so he rode into one of their holy places and hurled his spear at the statues there. When the heathens saw that nothing dreadful happened, many decided that he was right and became Christians.

The Beginning of a New Religion

Soon after AD600,* in the land of Arabia, a man called Muhammad was preaching a new religion. He believed in Allah, the "One God". By the time of his death, most people in Arabia followed his religion and called him the Prophet.

In Europe, most people in the Roman Empire were Christians. But when the Empire was invaded, many of them began worshipping other gods. The eastern part of the Roman Empire (called the Byzantine Empire) was not invaded and stayed Christian.

MUSLIM EMPIRE

EMPIRE OF CHARLEMAGNE

BYZANTINE EMPIRE

1 Islam — Page from Koran.

The teachings of Muhammad were collected and written down in a book called the Koran. His faith became known as Islam and his followers were called Muslims.

2

The caliphs, who were Muhammad's successors, believed that everyone should become Muslims. They fought many wars to spread their faith and conquered a great empire.

3

These Muslims are making a pilgrimage to Mecca, the home of Muhammad. All Muslims are meant to visit Mecca at least once in their lives.

Muslims eat and drink only at night during the month they call Ramadan. Good Muslims also give money to the poor.

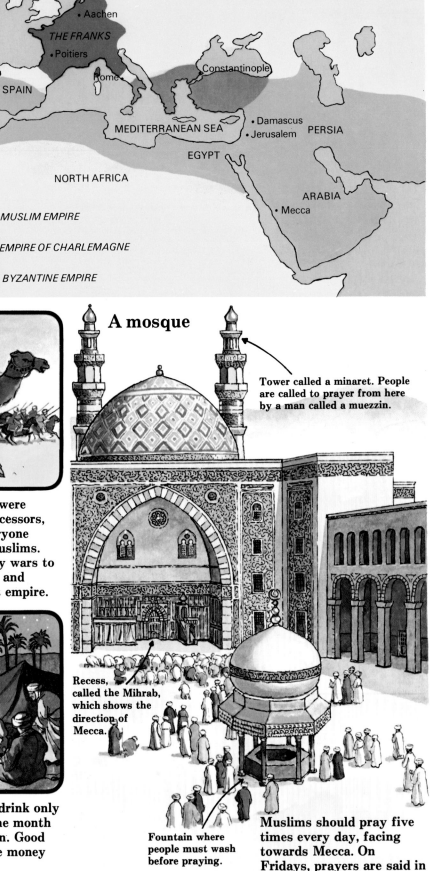

A mosque

Tower called a minaret. People are called to prayer from here by a man called a muezzin.

Recess, called the Mihrab, which shows the direction of Mecca.

Fountain where people must wash before praying.

Muslims should pray five times every day, facing towards Mecca. On Fridays, prayers are said in buildings, like this, called mosques.

* AD stands for two Latin words. Dates with AD next to them are that number of years after the birth of Christ.

Christians in Europe

1 The Christian Church in western Europe was led by the Pope, seen here with one of his priests. Many popes sent out missionaries to persuade people to become Christians.

2 Some missionaries were killed by the people they tried to convert. It was several hundred years before people in Europe accepted Christianity as their religion.

3 The Muslims began to invade southern Europe. In AD732, Charles Martel, king of a people called the Franks, stopped their advance by defeating them at the Battle of Poitiers.

4 This is Roderigo of Bivar, who was known as El Cid, which means "The Lord". He helped to keep the Muslims out of northern Spain and became a great Christian hero.

5 In AD768, Charlemagne (Charles the Great) became King of the Franks. He conquered a lot of Europe and became its first great leader since the fall of the Roman Empire.

6 Charlemagne forced the people he conquered to become Christians, and fought the Muslims in Spain. On Christmas Day AD800, Pope Leo III crowned him Holy Roman Emperor.

7

This gold image of Charlemagne was made to put his skull in.

After Charlemagne's death his empire was divided. The Holy Roman Emperors ruled only the German-speaking peoples of Europe from then on, but were still very powerful.

8 Emperors and popes often quarrelled over power. After one quarrel, Pope Gregory VII kept Henry IV waiting in the snow outside Canossa Castle for three days before he would forgive him. Quarrels between other emperors and popes resulted in long, bitter wars in Germany and Italy.

Key dates

AD570/632	Life of **Muhammad**.
AD622	First year of the Muslim calendar.
AD630	Mecca surrendered to Muhammad.
AD635	Muslims captured Damascus.
AD637/642	Muslims conquered Persia.
AD638	Muslims captured Jerusalem.
AD641/642	Muslims conquered Egypt.
By AD700	All North Africa conquered by Muslims.
AD732	Battle of Poitiers.
AD768/814	Reign of **Charlemagne**.
AD800	**Charlemagne** crowned Holy Roman Emperor.
AD1077	Meeting at Canossa between **Henry IV** and **Gregory VII**.
AD1043/1099	Life of **El Cid**.

Life in Viking Times

In Denmark, Norway and Sweden there lived a people called the North or Norsemen. They were farmers, fishermen and traders. Norsemen who sailed abroad were called Vikings. Some Vikings settled in France and became known as Normans.

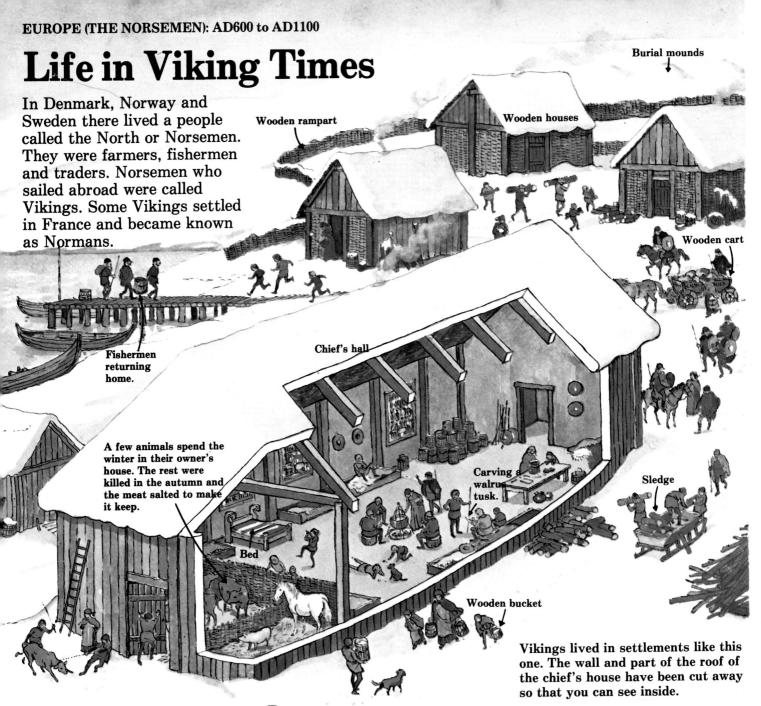

Burial mounds

Wooden rampart

Wooden houses

Wooden cart

Fishermen returning home.

Chief's hall

A few animals spend the winter in their owner's house. The rest were killed in the autumn and the meat salted to make it keep.

Carving a walrus tusk.

Sledge

Bed

Wooden bucket

Vikings lived in settlements like this one. The wall and part of the roof of the chief's house have been cut away so that you can see inside.

Carvings

The Vikings were skilled wood-carvers and metal-workers. This carved wooden head is from a wagon.

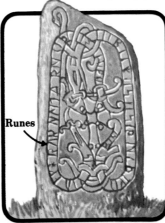

Runes

Memorial stones to the dead were sometimes set up. These usually had letters called runes carved on them.

A burial

This is the grave of a Viking warrior. Later it will be covered with earth. His possessions, including his animals and sometimes even a slave, were buried with him. The Vikings believed that dead warriors went to "Valhalla", the hall of the gods.

Viking raiders

The men row when they are setting off and landing and when there is not enough wind for sailing.

When they are out of sight of land they steer by the Pole Star and the sun.

Steering oar

Ropes at bottom corners turn sail to catch the wind.

The Vikings were sailors, warriors and adventurers. At first they robbed and plundered other lands. Later they settled in many parts of Europe, including Iceland.

From Iceland they went to Greenland and from there they are thought to have reached America. Long poems, called sagas, were written about brave Viking heroes.

The Vikings in France (Normans) were great soldiers. In AD1066, William, Duke of Normandy conquered England. Another group set out and conquered Sicily and part of Italy.

Where the Vikings went

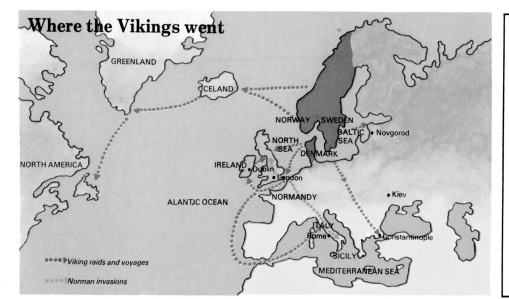

GREENLAND

ICELAND

NORWAY   SWEDEN

NORTH SEA   BALTIC SEA   • Novgorod

DENMARK

IRELAND   • Dublin

NORTH AMERICA

• London

ATLANTIC OCEAN   NORMANDY

ITALY   • Kiev
Rome

Constantinople

SICILY

MEDITERRANEAN SEA

••••• Viking raids and voyages

••••• Norman invasions

Key dates

AD793/900	Great Viking raids on British Isles and northern France.
AD862	Viking settlers in Kiev and Novgorod in Russia.
AD870/930	Iceland colonized by Vikings.
AD900/911	Normandy settled by Vikings.
AD960	**Harald Bluetooth**, King of Denmark, converted to Christianity.
AD1000	Vikings reached America.
AD1016	**Knut** became King of England.
AD1066	**William of Normandy** (William the Conqueror), descendant of Viking settlers, conquered England. Other Normans conquered part of Italy.

Kings, Knights and Castles

All the countries of Europe were organized in roughly the same way in the Middle Ages. A king or emperor ruled a whole country and owned all the land.

The king sometimes needed support or money for a particular plan. So he called a meeting of his nobles, bishops and specially chosen knights and townsmen to discuss it with him. This was the beginning of parliaments.

The king divided his land amongst his most important men. In return, they did "homage" to him. This meant that they knelt in front of him and promised to serve him and fight for him, whenever they were needed. These men were the nobles.

Each noble divided his land among knights who did homage to him. Peasants served a noble or knight and, in return, were allowed to live on his land. This arrangement of exchanging land for services is called the "feudal system".

Castles were uncomfortable places to live. They were damp, cold and draughty. Early castles had no glass in the windows and there was no running water. They were lit by torches made of twigs or rushes.

Kings and nobles built castles to protect themselves against enemies. These might be foreign invaders, other nobles or even rebellious peasants. We have taken away two walls so you can see inside.

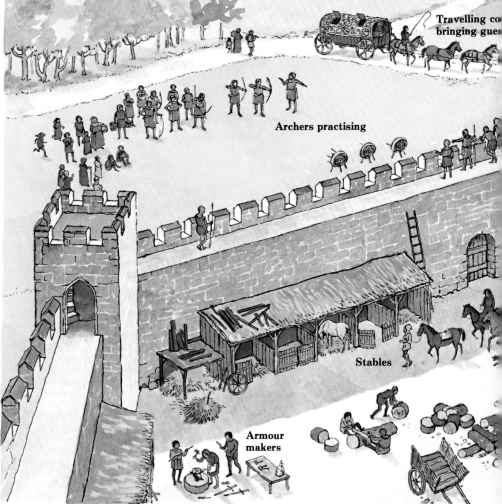

Travelling co
bringing gue

Archers practising

Stables

Armour
makers

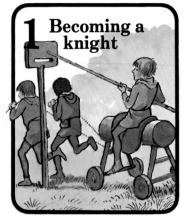

1 Becoming a knight

A boy who wanted to be a knight was sent to a noble's house as a page. He was taught to fight and to behave properly.

2 When he was older he became a squire. It was his job to serve a knight and to follow him into battle. Here is a squire with his knight.

3 If he proved himself to be worthy of the honour, a noble, perhaps even the king, would "knight" the young man.

4 The new knight's father or another noble usually gave him some land with peasants and villages. This was called a manor.

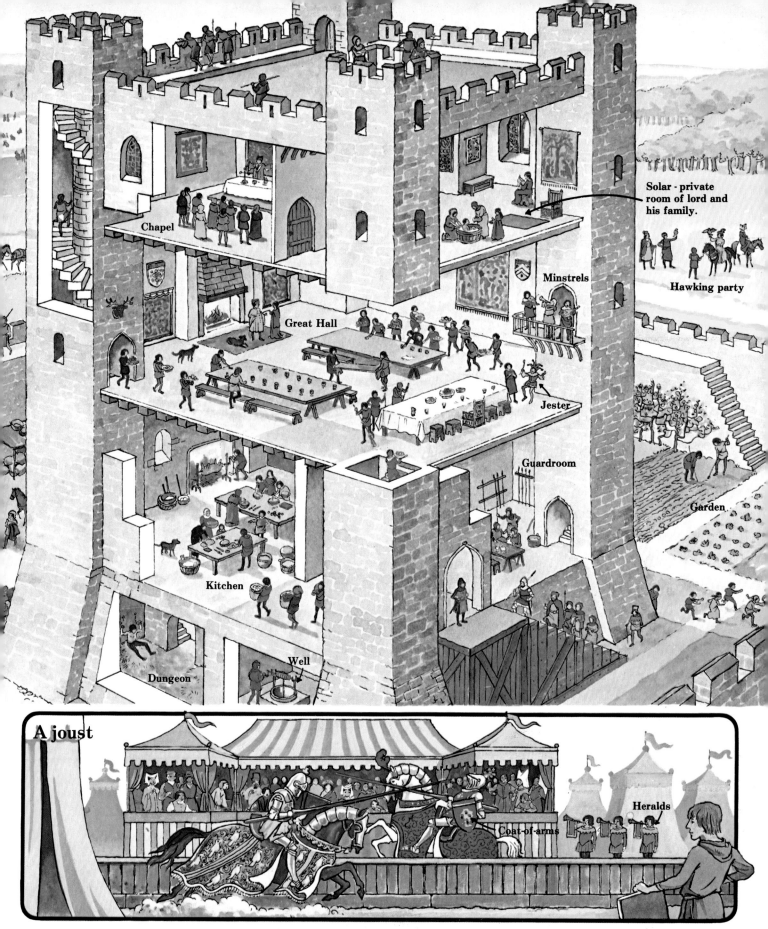

Solar - private room of lord and his family.

Hawking party

Chapel

Minstrels

Great Hall

Jester

Guardroom

Garden

Kitchen

Well

Dungeon

A joust

Heralds

Coat-of-arms

To keep in practice for battle, knights took part in specially organized fights. These were called tournaments or jousts. At a joust, two knights on horseback charged at each other with long lances, and tried to knock each other to the ground. Each noble family had a "coat-of-arms", which was painted on their shields, so they could be recognized in armour.

A knight wore a ribbon, badge or scarf belonging to his favourite lady. This was called her "favour". If he won he brought great honour to her as well as to himself.

Village Life

In the Middle Ages, most people in Europe lived in villages. Each village was controlled by the Lord of the Manor. It usually had three fields, divided into strips, which the lord allowed the villagers to farm. They paid him by working for him and by giving him some of the food they grew.

All the peasants can use the common. They can graze their animals here and gather wood and berries.

The ford is a shallow part of the stream, where people can cross.

Fisherman. The Church said people should always eat fish on Fridays.

Ford

The villagers are holding a fair. This is their only chance to buy goods from outside the village. Jugglers, acrobats and musicians have come to perform at the fair.

Priest's house

Dancing bear

Merchants are coming to the fair to buy the villagers' wool.

Black death

Villagers harvesting wheat. Next year they will grow barley here.

In AD1348, a ship from the East arrived in an Italian port. Some sick sailors came ashore bringing with them a terrible disease, known as the Plague or Black Death.

The Plague quickly spread across Europe because people knew little about medicine or the need to be clean. About one person in every three died from it.

The Lord of the Manor lives here in the Manor House.

Lord of the Manor going hunting. The peasants are forbidden to kill any game animals because that would spoil the lord's hunting.

Stray animals are put in a "pound" and their owners have to pay a fine before they can get them out.

Everyone has their grain ground into flour at the village mill.

In this field barley is growing. Next year it will be left unplanted.

Hole for smoke to come out.

Ale house

Blacksmith

Stocks

Roof made of straw or reeds. This is called thatch.

Vegetable plot and garden.

Spinning wool

This field has been left fallow (unplanted) this year. This will make it more fertile for wheat next year.

Tinker coming to fair to mend and sell metal pots and pans.

9

Towns and Trade

This is what towns looked like in the Middle Ages. The streets were made of earth or cobbles and were narrow and dirty. There were no underground drains so people threw their rubbish into the street. Rich merchants built their houses of stone but most houses were made of wood, so fire was always a great danger. Towns were very small by modern standards and were surrounded by high stone walls.

University

Picture sign shows what the shop sells.

As trade increased and towns grew richer, townsmen wanted to organize their own affairs. Many towns obtained a charter from the king or local lord.

1 Guilds

Each trade and craft had its own guild. The guild organized its members by fixing prices and standards of workmanship.

2

A boy who wanted to learn a trade was "apprenticed" to a master. He lived in his master's house and worked in his shop.

3

After seven years he made a special piece of work called a masterpiece. If it was good enough he could join the guild.

4

The mayor and corporation, who ran the city, were chosen from the most important members of each of the guilds.

5

When the population increased men could not find places as guild members so they had to work for others for wages.

Mystery plays

On special holidays each guild acted different scenes from the Bible. These were called "mystery" plays. The guilds acted their plays on wagons called pageants, which they moved around the town between each performance. Many people could not read so the plays helped them to get to know the stories in the Bible. In many towns the guild which did the best play won a prize.

1 Trade

Banker

The first bankers were rich merchants who lent money to people wanting to organize trading expeditions.

2

Spices, jewels and silks were brought to Europe from India and China. Italian merchants controlled this trade.

3

Goods were carried overland by packhorses. Most roads were very bad and there were often bandits in lonely areas.

4

Sea travel was also difficult and dangerous. Sailors steered by the stars and tried to keep close to the land whenever they could.

The Church

1

The head of the Church in western Europe, the Pope, was elected by cardinals (the highest rank of priests) at a meeting called a conclave.

Cardinals

Pope

At one time there were three rival popes who all claimed to have been elected by a conclave. This argument was called the Great Schism.

2

Everyone went to church. All the services were in Latin, although only the priests and highly-educated people understood it.

3

Few people could read and write, except priests, so kings used priests as secretaries and advisers. Priests of high rank were summoned to parliament.

4

No one in Europe had discovered how to print books. All books were written by hand by monks and were often decorated with bright colours and gold leaf.

Pilgrims

5

People who refused to believe everything that the Church taught were called heretics and were sometimes burnt to death. Joan of Arc was burnt as a heretic but later people decided she was a saint.

6

Bodies of saints or holy objects were often put into jewelled containers called reliquaries. These were treated with great respect and people worshipped in front of them.

Some people went on journeys to holy places to show their devotion to God, to be forgiven for some sin or cured of an illness. These journeys were called pilgrimages.

Life in a nunnery

Some people chose to give their lives completely to God's service and to live apart from the rest of the world. Women who did this were called nuns and lived in nunneries. Men were called monks and lived in monasteries. Trainee monks and nuns were called novices.

Nuns are always ready to give food and beds to tired pilgrims and travellers.

Abbess's house

Peasants from the village working on nunnery lands.

Nun giving food to some poor people

Stables

Visitors' houses

Cloisters where nuns take exercise.

Dormitory

Chapter House where meetings are held.

Refectory, where the nuns eat their meals. In some nunneries they eat in silence while a religious book is read to them.

Hospice where nuns look after people who are ill.

Nuns and monks promised to obey their superiors, to give up everything they owned and never to marry. Each day was divided into special times for prayer, study and work.

Like any Lord of the Manor, a nunnery had land. Rich people often left land and money to the nuns when they died, so that the nuns would pray for them. Some nunneries became extremely rich.

Key dates

AD1181/1226 Life of **St Francis of Assisi**.
AD1100s and 1200s Quarrels between popes and emperors led to wars in Germany and Italy.
AD1265/1321 The poet **Dante** lived.
AD1273 **Rudolf of Habsburg** became King of the Germans. His family ruled until 1918.
AD1307/1314 The Knights Templar were disbanded.
AD1337/1453 The "**Hundred Years**" **War** between England and France.
AD1370/1417 The Great Schism.
AD1380/1422 Quarrels between French nobles helped the English in the war.
AD1412/1431 Life of **Joan of Arc**. She led the French to victory in the war but was then burnt as a heretic.

Wars Between Religions

When invaders overran the western part of the Roman Empire, the eastern (Byzantine) half survived. The city of Constantinople was its capital.

These are priests of the Byzantine "Orthodox" Church. Over the years, eastern Christians developed slightly different beliefs from those of the west.

Between AD632 and 645 Muslims conquered part of the Byzantine Empire. Here their caliph (ruler) enters Jerusalem. Later, emperors and caliphs made peace.

Many Christian pilgrims visited the Holy Land, where Jesus had lived. The Muslims allowed them to continue these visits.

The Crusades

In AD1095, Pope Urban II gave a sermon at Clermont in France. He inspired his listeners to go on a crusade (holy war).

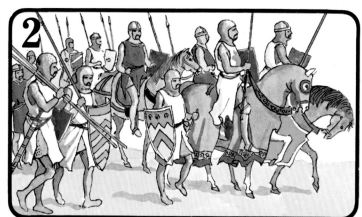

The Crusaders set out on the long and difficult journey to the Holy Land to win it back from the Muslims.

The leaders of the First Crusade were French noblemen but their followers came from many different countries.

The Crusaders arrived in Constantinople and met the Emperor. At first he was friendly but really he did not trust them.

The Muslims, under a great leader called Saladin, won back Jerusalem from the quarrelling Christians. Several new crusades set out from Europe to try to win it back.

The feeling between the Byzantines and the European Crusaders became so bad that one group of Crusaders attacked Constantinople itself and set up their own emperor.

Richard the Lionheart of England, Frederick II of Germany and St Louis of France tried to save Outremer but by AD1291 the Muslims had recaptured the Holy Land.

In the 11th century*, Seljuk Turks, who were also Muslims, arrived in the area from the east. They were very unfriendly to the Christians.

When the Turks defeated the Byzantines at the Battle of Manzikert, the western Christians felt they must go and fight to protect the Holy Land.

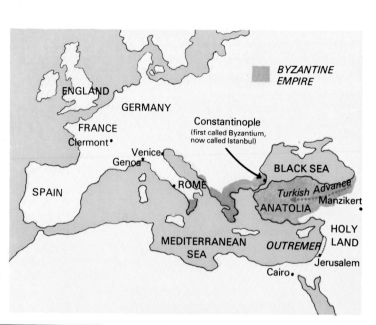

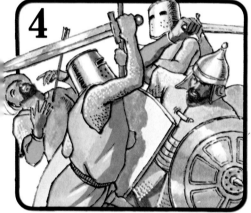

The Crusaders left Constantinople and went to fight the Muslims. They were very successful. The Holy Land became a Christian kingdom, called Outremer.

Special groups of soldier-monks were formed to care for pilgrims and to fight the Muslims. One knight from each of the three most important groups is shown here.

Some Crusaders settled in Outremer. When new Crusaders came out they were shocked to find the settlers quarrelling with each other but making friends with Muslim rulers.

The Byzantines won back Constantinople but the days of their wealth and power were over. In AD1453, with the help of cannons, the Turks finally captured the city.

How to spot a Crusader's tomb

Here is the tomb of a knight. His crossed legs show that he was a Crusader. Look out for a tomb like this if you go inside a church.

Key dates

AD632/645	Muslims seized parts of Byzantine Empire.
AD638	Caliph Omar took Jerusalem.
AD1000/1100	Turks invaded Byzantine Empire.
AD1071	Battle of Manzikert.
AD1095	Sermon at Clermont.
AD1096	First Crusade. Jerusalem taken. Outremer founded.
AD1187	**Saladin** took Jerusalem.
AD1191	Crusade of **Richard the Lionheart**.
AD1204	Sack of Constantinople.
AD1228/1244	**Emperor Frederick II** won back Jerusalem for a while.
AD1249/1270	Crusades of **St Louis**
AD1261	Byzantine Emperor recaptured Constantinople.
AD1291	The end of Outremer.
AD1453	Turks captured Constantinople. (End of Byzantine Empire.)

This means the 100 years between AD1000 and AD1100.

How Muslim People Lived

The Arabs were the first Muslims and they conquered a huge empire. At first the whole Muslim empire was ruled by one caliph, but later it split into several kingdoms. Life for the Muslims was often more advanced than life in Europe. After they had conquered the eastern provinces of the Roman Empire, they absorbed many of the ideas of ancient Greece and Rome. Trading made them wealthy, and this brought more comfort and luxury into their lives.

Many Arabs were nomads, who moved with their animals in search of water and pasture. They did not change their way of life even after they conquered their huge empire.

Peasants in Muslim lands went on working their fields. Much of the land was hot and dry and they had to work hard to keep it watered.

Muslim cities

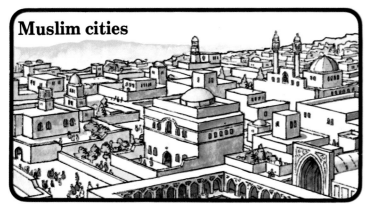

Houses in Muslim cities were often covered with white plaster, which helped to keep them cool. They faced inwards on to open courtyards, which provided shade. The streets were usually narrow and there were few open spaces except around the mosques.

Market

Towns usually had a souq (market). The streets where it was held were often roofed over. Shops in one street usually sold the same kind of goods.

Baths

Palaces and many private houses had baths and there were also public baths. They were copied from the designs of Roman baths.

1 Learning

Arabic writing

Arabic numbers

Our numbers

The Muslims developed a way of writing which read from right to left. Their system of numbers was simpler than the Roman figures used in Europe.

Arab astronomers

Muslim scholars studied Greek and Roman learning. They were especially interested in mathematics, the stars, geography, law, religion and medicine.

The Arabs made complicated instruments, like this one, which measured the position of ships at sea, by looking at the stars. This instrument is called an astrolabe.

Hospital

Muslim doctors followed ancient Greek methods of treating the sick. Hospitals were built to care for people who needed special treatment.

3 Muslim rulers built themselves huge palaces, like this one. These were beautifully decorated by skilled craftsmen, and were very comfortable, compared with European castles built at this time. They usually had gardens set out in patterns around fountains. Life in these palaces was very formal, with lots of ceremonies.

Harem windows

4 Part of a house was set aside for women only. This was called the harem. No man from outside the family could enter it. In the street, Muslim women wore veils.

Arab traders

Arab dhow

Trading played an important part in Muslim life. Arabs travelled to many different countries to find new customers. By sea they travelled in fast ships, called dhows. Some Arabs still use dhows today.

On land, merchants travelled by camel in groups called caravans. On main routes, caravansarays (shelters) were built at a day's journey from each other. Travellers could spend the night there.

Muslim art

Close-up of tiles

Tiles

Carpet

Incense burner

Their religion did not allow Muslim artists to make sculptures of the human figure. They used patterns, flowers, animals and birds as decoration. Tiles were often used for decorating buildings.

Muslim craftsmen were famous for the manufacture of beautiful carpets and for their metal work. The bronze lion, shown above, was used for holding burning incense. Crusaders who returned to the west took treasures like these back with them. The work of Muslim craftsmen became popular in Europe.

Genghis Khan and his Empire

The Mongols were nomads who wandered across the plains of Asia with their herds of horses. From AD1206, a chief called Temujin overpowered all the Mongol tribes and conquered a huge empire. He became known as Ghengis Khan, the Great Prince. His sons raided Europe and his grandson, Kubilai Khan, conquered China. The Mongols were then weakened by family quarrels and fierce resistance. Later, a chief called Tamerlane* conquered an empire of his own and invaded India.

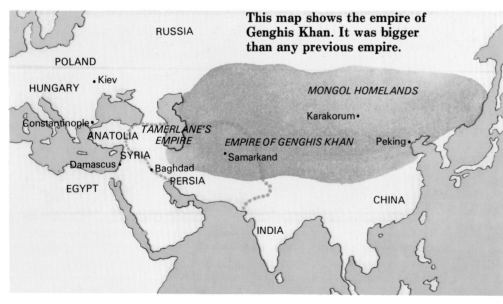

Muslim city being destroyed by Mongol raiders.

Mongols fought on horseback, using lances or bows and arrows.

Mongol commander. The Mongol army was very well-disciplined and could travel vast distances very quickly.

Here the Mongols are moving off after destroying an enemy city. The Mongols were very cruel to their enemies. Millions of people were killed or made slaves.

This map shows the empire of Genghis Khan. It was bigger than any previous empire.

RUSSIA

POLAND

HUNGARY

Kiev

Constantinople

ANATOLIA

TAMERLANE'S EMPIRE

Damascus

SYRIA

Baghdad

PERSIA

EGYPT

MONGOL HOMELANDS

Karakorum

EMPIRE OF GENGHIS KHAN

Samarkand

Peking

CHINA

INDIA

A friar visits the Mongols

A Christian friar, called William of Rubruck, was sent by St Louis of France to visit the Mongols. The Mongols had their own gods, but several of their

*Tamerlane is sometimes known as Tamburlaine.

Slaves

The yurts (tents) are packed up and put on horses.

Chief's tent being carried by ox-drawn cart.

Genghis Khan organized his empire very efficiently. He drew up a clear law code called the Yasa, encouraged trade, punished bandits and started a messenger service.

Some Mongols settled in the newly conquered lands and built cities. Others continued to live as nomads in tents. There are Mongols who still live this way today.

princes had married Christian princesses. The Christians thought the Mongols would help them fight the Muslims, but this never happened.

1 Tamerlane

This is the Mongol chief Timur the Lame, known in Europe as Tamerlane. He ruled his empire from the city of Samarkand.

2

This is the building in Samarkand where Tamerlane was buried. Russian archaeologists have opened his tomb.

3

By using modern methods scientists built up a face on his skull, so that we now know what he looked like.

Princes and Temples

1 India was divided into kingdoms ruled by wealthy princes. They built themselves luxurious palaces and kept musicians and dancers to entertain them.

2 Indian villagers worked hard to keep their fields watered for growing rice. Each village was run by a headman who carried out the orders of the local ruler.

3 Indians did most of their trade with Arabs. They sold silks, ivory, pearls, spices and perfumes and bought Arab horses, which were especially beautiful and could run fast.

4 Many people, both inside and outside India, had accepted the teachings of the Buddha. Pilgrims, like this Chinese monk, travelled a long way to visit sacred Buddhist shrines.

5 The ancient Hindu faith became popular again. There were many gods and goddesses but the god Shiva, shown above, was one of the most important ones.

6 Hindus believe that all rivers come from the gods. The river Ganges, shown above, is especially holy. For thousands of years they have bathed in it to wash away their sins.

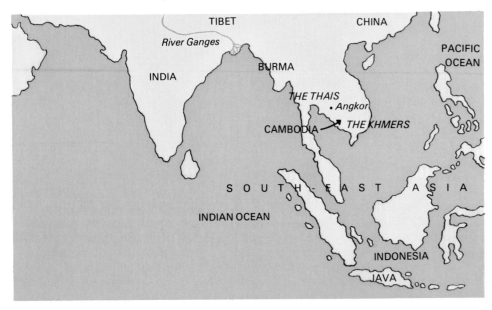

Indian ideas in other countries

Indian religions, ideas and ways of life spread to other countries, especially in South-East Asia. This is a Buddhist temple at Borobudur on the island of Java in Indonesia.

Angkor

One of the countries that was influenced by Indian ideas was Cambodia. In the ninth century a people called the Khmers rose to power there. They worshipped their own kings as gods on earth, but they also worshipped Hindu gods and built huge temples, like this one at Angkor. In AD1431 a people called the Thais invaded Cambodia. The great cities and temples of the Khmers were abandoned and the jungle grew up and covered them.

In AD1296 a Chinese visitor to Cambodia saw a procession like this and wrote an account of it.

Pictures, like this, were cut into the stone of Angkor. They tell us about the battles, on land and rivers, fought by the Khmers against their enemies the Chams and Thais.

The stone carvings at Angkor also tell us about the everyday life of the Khmers. This picture shows two men and their friends getting ready to watch a fight between two cockerels.

Silk and Spice Traders

In AD589 a new dynasty (family line) of emperors, called the Sui, began to rule China. They brought peace to the country after a time of long and difficult wars between rival Chinese groups.

Civil servants helped the Emperor to rule. They had to take exams before they were given jobs in government. In the countryside, the nobles, who owned most of the land, gradually became more powerful.

Buddhism had spread from India in the first century AD and was very popular. But many people still believed in the teachings of Confucius and the Taoist religion. At times Buddhists were persecuted.

A trading city in China

Some merchants travelled by sea to Africa and the Middle East.

Chinese inventions

The Chinese were the inventors of several things that were unknown to the rest of the world at this time.

They discovered how to make porcelain, a very hard, fine type of china.

At this time, the Chinese were using compasses to find their way across land and sea. This one is made of lacquered wood.

By the 10th century they were using wooden blocks to print books. This is probably the oldest printed page in the world.

Gunpowder was first used for fireworks. By the 13th century the Chinese were also using it for bombs and other weapons.

2 Chinese craftsmen were very skilful. At the time when the T'ang family were emperors (AD618/906) they made especially fine pottery figures of animals and servants. These were placed in tombs.

3 In AD1279 the Mongols, led by the great Kubilai Khan, overran China, which they then ruled for nearly 100 years.

Key dates

AD589/618	Sui Dynasty ruled.
AD618/906	T'ang Dynasty ruled. Buddhism very popular.
AD960/1279	Sung Dynasty ruled. Growth of trade. Mongols started attacking northern frontier.
AD1279/1368	Mongols ruled China.
AD1276/1292	**Marco Polo's** trip to China.
AD1368	Mongol rulers overthrown.
AD1368/1644	Ming Dynasty ruled.

Silk, porcelain (fine china) and carved jade were taken to the west and traded for silver and gold. Many cities grew rich because of this trade.

This caravan of camels is setting out with goods destined for the Middle East and Europe.

1 Marco Polo

Many foreign merchants, especially Arabs, came to China to trade. Later, a few adventurous Europeans arrived. Two of the European merchants who visited China were the brothers,

Niccolo and Maffeo Polo, from Venice. On their second visit they took Maffeo's young son, Marco. Here they are meeting Kubilai Khan, the Mongol emperor of China.

2 Marco Polo travelled around Kubilai Khan's empire for nearly 17 years. When he returned home, he wrote a book about his travels. This is the first page of his book.

Land of the Samurai

Japan is a group of islands off the coast of China. We know little about its early history because the Japanese had no writing until it was introduced from China in the fifth century AD. The Buddhist religion also came from China and won many followers, although Japan's ancient religion, Shinto, was still popular. Japanese arts, crafts, laws, taxes and the organization of government were also based on Chinese ideas.

SEA OF JAPAN

JAPAN

• Heian (now Kyoto)

PACIFIC OCEAN

This is part of the Imperial city, Heian, later called Kyoto. The emperor was at the centre of power, but noble clans (families) gradually took over and ruled for him. Many emperors retired to Buddhist monasteries. As "Cloistered Ex-Emperors", some re-established their power for a time.

Legally all the land in Japan was owned by the emperor. He allowed farmers, like these, to use it in return for taxes and services. Later, the nobles began to acquire their own private lands because the Emperor was not strong enough to stop them. Many battles were fought about the possession of land and nobles gave it to their supporters as rewards.

This is Yoritomo, military leader and the chief of the Minamoto clan. In AD1192 he began to use the title "Shogun". This became the name for the head of government and was passed from father to son.

Poetry

Poetry was popular, especially among the people at court. People made trips to look at the cherry blossom and see the maple leaves turning red. This inspired them to recite and write poems. There were several famous women poets.

Novels

The Japanese liked novels. This is Murasaki Shikibu, a court lady, who wrote a famous novel called *The Tale of Genji*.

Armour making

Japanese warriors wore suits of armour made of tough leather strips. This is an armourer's shop where the suits were made.

Curved swords made by highly-skilled swordsmiths.

Helmets were made to look like the face of the wearer.

Armour made from tough leather strips.

The Mongol Invasion Scroll

The Mongol ruler of China, Kubilai Khan, twice tried to invade Japan, but his men were driven back by the Samurai and by storms called Kamikaze. This scroll tells the story.

Japanese warriors were called Samurai. They fought for the nobles and had to be absolutely loyal to them. They were rewarded with land and wealth, but were expected to die for their lords if necessary.

The Samurai fought hand-to-hand battles, skilfully wielding deadly two-handed swords. Before attacking, each Samurai would shout his own name and tell of the bravery of his ancestors, hoping to strike fear into the heart of his enemy.

Key dates

AD538	Buddhist religion introduced to Japan.
AD794	Capital city moved from Nara to Heian (now called Kyoto).
AD794/1185	Period of Japanese history called Heian.
AD851/1115	Fujiwara clan controlled government.
AD1115/1160	Some power taken by "Cloistered Ex-Emperors".
AD1180/1185	Taira and Minamoto clans fought for control of government.
AD1192	**Minamoto Yoritomo** took the title of Shogun.
AD1185/1333	Period of Japanese history called Kamakura.
AD1274/1281	Mongol invasions.
AD1333/1336	Period of rule by the emperor
AD1392/1573	Period of Japanese history called Ashikaga.

Kingdoms, Traders and Tribes

In AD639, Arabs, inspired by their new religion, Islam, invaded Egypt and then north Africa. They traded with the local people and brought new wealth to the area.

South of the Sahara, the land was often difficult to clear and live in. There were also dangerous diseases there. As people learnt how to make strong tools from iron, tribes were able to progress further south, clearing and farming the land as they went.

MEDITERRANEAN SEA

MOROCCO

THE SAHARA

Timbuktu

KINGDOM OF MALI

A F R I C A

River Niger

River Congo

MUSLIM EMPIRE

ATLANTIC OCEAN

African king

KALAHARI DESERT

1 West African kingdoms

Arab traders began to make regular journeys across the Sahara. They bought gold and salt from West Africa and sold it in busy Mediterranean ports.

2 Trade made the local Africans very rich. They built magnificent cities full of palaces and mosques. The most famous city was Timbuktu shown here.

3

Arab visitors

Portuguese explorers

Some of the West African rulers had large kingdoms. One of the most important was Mali. Several Arabs who travelled to these kingdoms kept records of their visits. They were very impressed by the luxury they found, especially at court. Here, some Arabs are meeting an African king.

From AD1420 onwards, Prince Henry of Portugal, known as "the Navigator", organized expeditions to explore the West African coast and trade with the Africans.

A great ancient civilisation once existed here in Egypt.

EGYPT
Cairo
NUBIA
ARABIA
River Nile
RED SEA
ETHIOPIA
PERSIAN GULF
Kilwa
Zambesi
INDIAN OCEAN

East African traders

Arab traders bought gold, iron, ivory and coconuts from Kilwa, and other east coast towns, and shipped them to India and China in their fast dhows (ships).

Church in Ethiopia

This picture shows a Christian church in Ethiopia. In the north, only Ethiopia managed to withstand the Muslim invasion and to keep its Christian faith.

The first giraffe in China

This Chinese picture shows a giraffe arriving in China from Africa in AD1415.

Life in the south

In the south different tribes adopted different ways of life.

In the Kalahari Desert the Bushmen hunted animals for their food.

Pygmies lived in tropical jungles, hunting animals and gathering berries and fruits.

Tribes living in the open plains of the east and south kept animals and farmed the land.

People who knew how to make iron tools were very useful to their tribes.

27

Life in North and South America

At this time there were many separate groups of people living in different parts of the huge continent of America. In the forests, mountains, plains, deserts and jungles and in the frozen north, people found ways of surviving by hunting, fishing, gathering, and later farming. The people of North America did not have a system of writing, but archaeologists have found remains of their settlements, which tell us something about their lives.

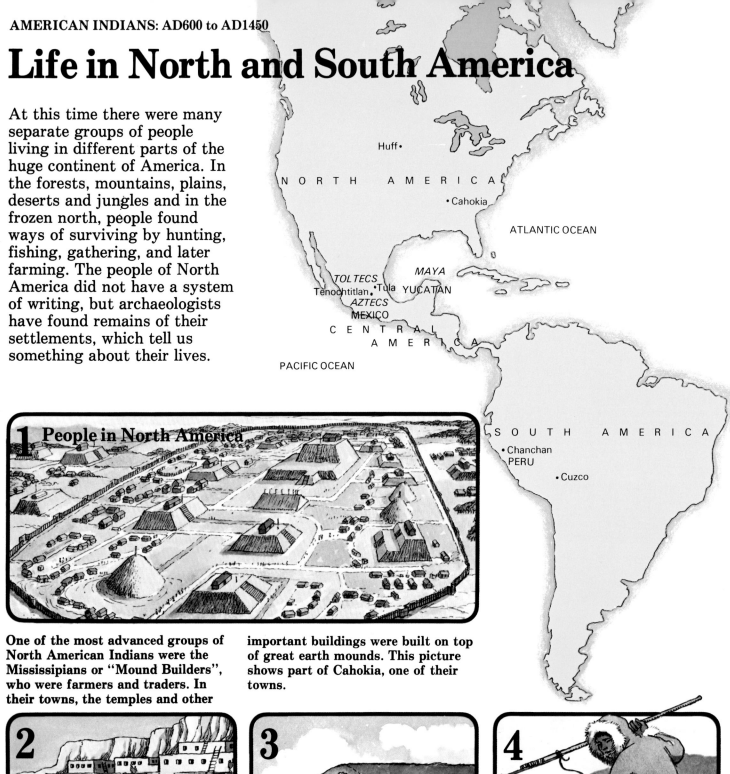

1 People in North America

One of the most advanced groups of North American Indians were the Mississipians or "Mound Builders", who were farmers and traders. In their towns, the temples and other important buildings were built on top of great earth mounds. This picture shows part of Cahokia, one of their towns.

2

Underground rooms (kivas) were used for religious ceremonies.

Some Indian farmers lived in "pueblos", towns made of stone and mud. The houses were sometimes as high as five floors and were built in canyon walls.

3

At Huff, on the plains, traces of a village of more than 100 wooden houses, like this, have been found. The village was surrounded by a ditch and palisade (wooden fence).

4

Eskimos learnt how to live in the intense cold of the far north. They hunted caribou, seals and whales and also fished and trapped birds.

28

Mountain farmers in Peru

What the Indians made

The people in Peru were skilled potters and metal-workers and expert weavers. Some of the cloth they made has lasted to the present day and is still brightly-coloured. Each of the objects shown above was made by a different people.

The first American farmers we know about lived in the area that is now Peru. They grew maize, vegetables, cotton, tobacco and a drug called coca. Later they built terraces on the mountainside, so that they could grow crops even on the steep slopes of the Andes. Alpacas and llamas provided wool and carried heavy loads.

Towns

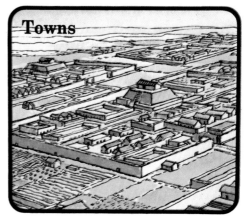

At first, the people of Peru had small settlements. Later they built great monuments and cities, such as the Chimu peoples' capital of Chanchan, shown above.

The Incas

These men are Inca warriors. The Incas were a tribe who lived in the mountains of Peru. The first Inca ruler probably lived about AD1200.

In 1438 a man called Pachacutec became their king and they spread out from the city of Cuzco, their capital, to conquer a huge empire.

Key dates

North America
AD500/1500   The Mound Builders or Mississipians lived.
AD1400/1600 People living at Huff.

South America
AD200/900   Period of Peruvian civilisation called the "Classic Period".
AD1100/1438 Chimu people living at Chanchan.
AD1200   **Manco Capac** ruled the Incas.
AD1438/1471 **Pachacutec** ruled the Incas.

Central America
700BC/AD900 Maya living in Yucatan.
100BC   Zapotecs living on the south coast.
AD750/990   The Toltec Empire.
AD1325   Aztecs known to be at Tenochtitlan.

29

The Aztecs

1

One of the earliest and greatest peoples of Central America were the Maya. This picture shows a procession of Mayan musicians.

2

Archaeologists have recently discovered, in the same area, more about a people called the Toltecs. This is a temple in Tula, their capital city.

3

This is an Aztec warrior. The Aztecs probably came from western Mexico before they settled at Tenochtitlan and conquered all the land around it.

Aztec numbers

1   20   400   8,000

20+20+20
+20+20=100

Blanket   400

Bag of
cocoa   ←2

100 bags
of cocoa   402 blankets

The Aztecs had a system of numbers, which meant they could count and keep records of their possessions. These are some of the symbols they used.

The market place

Dogs, fattened ready to be eaten.

Avocadoes

Tomatoes

Corn

Limes   Pineapples

Trading between themselves and with people from other towns was an important part of Aztec life. They had no money so they exchanged goods for others of equal value. This is called barter. Chocolate was a favourite drink, so cocoa beans, from which it was made, were always in demand. They were often used for making small payments. Jade and turquoise were more valuable than gold and silver.

Calendar

This picture shows the "New Fire Ceremony", which marked the beginning of a 52 year cycle. There were 18 months in each year.

Schools

Children were taught by their parents. At 15 the boys went to school. Special schools trained boys and girls as priests.

The city of Tenochtitlan

This is the capital city of the Aztecs. It was built on islands in the middle of a lake. The lake no longer exists and modern Mexico City is built on top of it.

The Aztecs worshipped many gods and goddesses. They built temples where they killed human beings and ripped out their hearts, in order to please these gods.

Temple of the Rain God

Human sacrifice

Temple of the War God (Chief Aztec god)

Lake

Temple

Emperor's palace

Temple of the Feathered Serpent, one of the Aztec gods

This wall called the Serpent Wall.

Aztecs playing "tlachtli", a game using a rubber ball.

Special boats collect waste.

Mosaic and feathers

How we know

Aztec craftsmen produced beautiful mosaic work, like this mask, which is covered with small pieces of precious turquoise.

Shields, like this one, were made of feathers. The Aztecs also used feathers for making head-dresses and cloaks.

The Aztecs used a form of picture-writing. It had not developed far enough to record complicated ideas but some religious teachings and history were recorded and have survived in books like the one above. Such a book is called a codex.

31

The Slav People

Many of the people who now live in Eastern Europe and Western Russia are Slavs. They settled in these places in the 700s, after centuries of wandering across Europe. In the west, the Slav people set up several kingdoms for themselves. In the south, they were ruled by a people called Bulgars. In the east, the Slav people settled with the Vikings, who called the area "Rus" and so gave us our name "Russia".

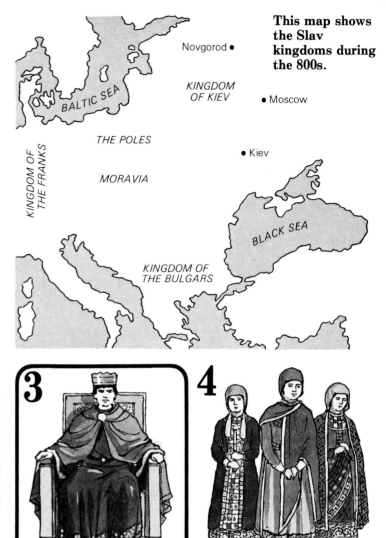

This map shows the Slav kingdoms during the 800s.

Novgorod •

BALTIC SEA

KINGDOM OF KIEV

• Moscow

THE POLES

KINGDOM OF THE FRANKS

MORAVIA

• Kiev

BLACK SEA

KINGDOM OF THE BULGARS

1

Some of the Slav kingdoms became very great and wealthy, but did not last very long. One of these was Moravia. This silver plaque is one of the few Moravian things to have survived.

2

The Southern and Eastern Slavs were converted to Christianity by Byzantine missionaries. This led them to copy the Byzantine art style, as in this picture.

3

The Western Slavs (present-day Poles and Czechs) also became Christians, but they joined the Roman Catholic instead of the Byzantine Church. This is the Polish king, Boleslav I.

4

Some Russian states became wealthy and powerful, and European kings began to take an interest in them. The most important was Kiev. Three of its Grand Prince's daughters married European kings.

5

At the beginning of the 13th century, Russia was invaded by a group of Mongols called Tartars. They destroyed many cities and made others, including the small town of Moscow, shown here, pay them tributes.

6

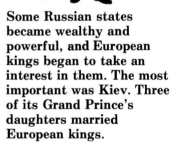

One Russian prince, called Alexander Nevsky, fought a great battle against the Tartars to save his city, Novgorod. He is still remembered as a great hero.

Kings, Popes and Princes

This picture shows a procession in Florence, the capital city of one of the greatest states in Italy. In the fifteenth century Florence was one of the great banking centres of Europe and was also famous as a clothmaking centre. The ruling family of Florence was called the Medici.

They were very wealthy and spent a lot of money on buying paintings and sculptures and having magnificent buildings constructed, which you can still see if you visit Florence. The most brilliant of the Medici princes was Lorenzo the Magnificent.

In the 15th century Italy was a collection of separate states. The central area around Rome was ruled by the Pope. Here the Pope is receiving a messenger from a foreign prince.

The Italian states were always fighting each other. In 1494 the French joined the fighting and soon the Spaniards and the emperor of the German states joined in as well.

Venice was one of the wealthiest states in Italy. Its ruler was called the "Doge". This is a portrait of one of the Doges, wearing the special Doge's hat.

Art and Learning

At the end of the 15th century, people in Europe began to take a great interest in art and learning, and to develop new ideas about the world. They started asking questions and doing experiments, instead of just accepting existing ideas.

People began to think that civilisation had been at its best in Ancient Greece and Rome, so they revived Greek and Roman ideas. The time became known as the "Renaissance", which means revival or rebirth. It began in Italy and gradually spread across Europe.

In the Renaissance, Italians began to be interested in the remains of Ancient Rome. They dug up statues and other treasures and made collections of them.

This is the city of Florence in Italy. The new ideas of the Renaissance began here and many of the most famous men of this time lived and worked in Florence.

1 Painting

Before the Renaissance, artists painted mainly religious scenes. Everything in their pictures looked flat and the people did not look very lifelike.

2

In the late 14th and early 15th centuries, painters began to try to make the people in their paintings look as much like living people as possible.

3

Besides painting religious subjects, Renaissance painters did pictures, like this one, of everyday life, and of stories from Ancient Greece and Rome.

Sculpture

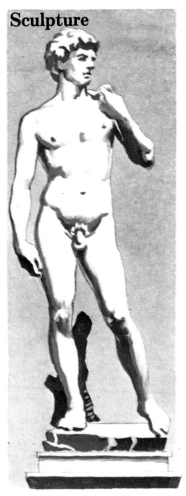

Sculptors were inspired by the statues of Ancient Greece and Rome. This marble statue was made by Michelangelo. He was also a painter, an architect and a poet.

4

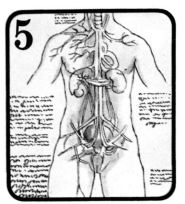

For the first time artists began to use live models to help them paint life-like people. This is Simonetta Vespucci, who modelled for the artist Botticelli.

5

Artists began to study nature and the human body to help them draw things more accurately. This sketch is from the notebook of Leonardo da Vinci.

6

Artists learned how to show distance in their paintings, making you feel you could walk into them. This is called "perspective".

1 Learning

Many new universities and schools were founded. The main subjects were Greek and Latin grammar. In England the new schools were called "grammar" schools.

2

Scholars studied texts in Greek, Latin and Hebrew. They were excited by the thoughts and ideas of ancient times. The invention of printing helped to spread these ideas.

3

Studying ancient Christian texts made some people, like this Dutch scholar called Erasmus, criticize the Church and its priests for being corrupt.

4

People also began to study politics. This is Machiavelli, an Italian who wrote a book about politics called "The Prince", in which he said that a ruler had to be ruthless.

Architecture

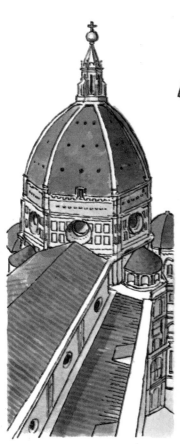

Architects built wonderful palaces and churches. They used domes and copied the style of Greek and Roman temples. The towers and spires of the Middle Ages went out of fashion.

A properly educated Renaissance person was expected to be able to:

understand and collect art,

write poetry,

play a musical instrument,

read and write Latin and Greek,

speak several languages,

fight if necessary,

take part in politics,

ride and be good at sports,

show good manners to everyone.

Science and Inventions

1

The new ideas of the Renaissance made people keen to question everything about the world around them. Some people began doing experiments to test their ideas.

2

People called "alchemists", however, tried to brew potions that would cure all ills, give eternal life and turn lead into gold.

3

One of the greatest men of the Renaissance was Leonardo da Vinci. He was a painter and an inventor and he thought a lot about making a flying machine. This is a model based on one of his designs which he worked out by watching birds fly. Leonardo also studied animals and human bodies to find out how they worked and he painted the very famous picture of the Mona Lisa.

4

The printing press was probably the most important invention of this time. The first one was made by a German called Johann Gutenberg. Books could now be produced quickly and cheaply, instead of having to be handwritten as before. This meant ideas and learning spread more quickly.

5

In England, people experimented with metals and learnt how to make cheap and reliable cannons out of cast-iron. These soon replaced the expensive bronze cannons that the Germans and Italians had been making.

6

There were very few clocks in the Middle Ages and these were usually huge ones on public buildings. The invention of springs made it possible to make watches that could be carried around and also small clocks that people could keep at home. Pendulum clocks were also invented at this time.

7

During the 16th century, the invention and improvement of instruments like these helped sailors to steer their ships more accurately. To make the most of these instruments a captain had to know the stars and be good at mathematics. Gradually, new and better maps were produced too.

Medicine

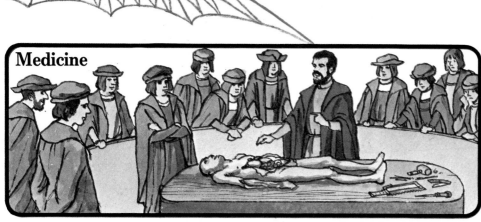

In 1543, a Belgian doctor called Andreas Vesalius published a book about how the human body worked. Here he is lecturing to his students at the university in Padua. William Harvey, another great doctor, discovered and proved that the heart pumps blood round the body.

The invention of microscopes made people realize for the first time that the world was full of minute creatures, too small to see unless they are magnified.

1 Ideas about the universe

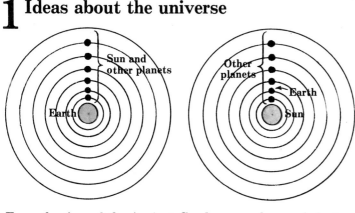

From the time of the Ancient Greeks onwards, people had believed that the Earth was the centre of the universe and that the Sun, Moon and stars moved round it. In 1543, the Polish astronomer, Copernicus, published a book showing that the Sun, not the Earth, was the centre of the universe. Many people refused to believe him.

The invention of the telescope in the early 17th century meant that people could get a better view of the stars and planets. The Italian scientist, Galileo, made a telescope strong enough to show the separate stars of the Milky Way. He supported Copernicus, but the Catholic Church forbade him to teach his theories.

The new interest in science led to the founding of scientific societies. Special places were built, like the Royal Observatory near London, for the study of stars.

The discoveries of the English scientist, Sir Isaac Newton, changed people's ideas about the universe. Here he is doing an experiment through which he discovered that white light is made up of different colours.

Key dates

AD1444/1510 Italian painter, **Botticelli**.
AD1452/1519 Italian artist/inventor **Leonardo da Vinci**.
AD1454 **Gutenberg** invented his printing press.
AD1466/1536 Dutch scholar **Erasmus**.
AD1469/1527 Italian writer **Machiavelli**.
AD1473/1543 Polish astronomer **Copernicus**.
AD1475/1564 Italian artist **Michelangelo**.
AD1514/1564 Belgian doctor **Vesalius**.
AD1564/1642 Italian astronomer **Galileo**.
AD1578/1657 English doctor **Harvey**.
AD1600 (approx.) Invention of telescope and microscope.
AD1642/1727 English scientist **Newton**.

New Ideas About Religion

The people of Western Europe were all Roman Catholics, but by AD1500, many were unhappy with the way the Church was being run. The Popes and many of the priests seemed interested only in wealth and power and set a bad example in the way they lived their lives: This led to a movement, which became known as the "Reformation", to change and reform the Christian Church. People who joined the movement were called "Protestants" because they were protesting about things that they thought were wrong.

In 1517 a German monk called Martin Luther nailed a list of 95 complaints about the Church and the way priests behaved, to the door of Wittenberg church in Germany.

Luther believed that everyone should be able to study God's message for themselves. So he translated the Bible from Latin into German. Versions in other languages quickly followed.

The Catholics fight back

The Pope called a meeting of churchmen at Trent in Italy. They laid down exactly what the beliefs and rules of the Catholic Church were and ordered complete obedience to them.

This is St Ignatius Loyola who founded the Society of Jesus. The members, who were known as Jesuits, tried to win Protestants back to the Catholic Church.

Many Protestants disapproved of decorated churches and destroyed those they took over. But the Catholics introduced an even more elaborate style, shown here, called Baroque.

Murders and executions

Holland was ruled by the Kings of Spain at this time. William of Orange led a revolt of the Dutch Protestants against the Spanish. He was murdered by a Catholic.

So many people in France became Protestants that the Catholics laid a plot. On 24 August 1572, the eve of St Bartholomew's Day, they murdered all the Protestants they could find in Paris.

Mary, Queen of Scots, was a Catholic. She plotted against Elizabeth I, the Protestant Queen of England, and was taken prisoner by the English. She was executed at Fotheringay Castle.

3 Luther was condemned by a Church court, but several German princes supported him. He also won followers across Europe.

4 King Henry VIII of England wanted to divorce his wife and marry Anne Boleyn. The Pope would not let him, so Henry made himself head of the Church in England.

5 Soon there were other religious leaders and the Protestants split into different groups. This is John Calvin, who set up a new Church in Geneva.

6 Priests on both sides were tortured and even hanged. Both Protestants and Catholics believed they were saving their opponents from hell by doing this.

4

In Spain, the most fiercely Catholic country in Europe, there was an organization called the Inquisition, which hunted out anyone who was not a good Catholic. The officers of the Inquisition used torture to make people confess their beliefs. Protestants who refused to become Catholics were burnt to death at special ceremonies called "Auto-da-fe" (Spanish for "acts of faith"), which were watched by huge crowds.

This is a map of Europe in about AD1600. It shows which areas were still Catholic and which had become Protestant.

Protestant

Catholic

ENGLAND

GERMAN STATES

Mixture of Catholic and Protestant

FRANCE

PORTUGAL

SPAIN

ITALIAN STATES

Key dates

AD1483/1546	Life of **Martin Luther**.
AD1517	Luther nailed 95 theses to Wittenburg church door.
AD1534	**Henry VIII** became head of the Church of England.
	Ignatius Loyola founded the Jesuits (Society of Jesus).
AD1536	**John Calvin** began work in Geneva.
AD1545/1563	The Council of Trent.
AD1555	Fighting between Catholics and Protestants in Germany ended by treaty called Peace of Augsburg.
AD1572	The Massacre of St. Bartholomew's Eve.
AD1584	**William of Orange** was assassinated.
AD1587	**Mary, Queen of Scots,** was executed.

War and Weapons

Guns were invented at the beginning of the 14th century. It was many years before they came into general use, but over the next few centuries they completely changed the way wars were fought. The knights and castles of the Middle Ages gradually disappeared. Their armour was no protection against bullets, so they could not get close enough to the enemy to use their swords and lances. Castle walls could not stand up to an attack of cannon balls.

From about 1300 onwards, archers started using longbows which were very effective against knights. They had a long range and were quite accurate.

Castles and walled towns had been very difficult to capture, but when cannons began to be used in the 15th century, even the thickest walls could be quickly battered down.

Armour and weapons were expensive. When peasants rebelled, as they often did in the 15th and 16th centuries, they had little chance against well-armed knights and nobles. This is a German knight charging a peasant.

When hand-guns were first invented they took a long time to load and were not very accurate. Pikemen were positioned next to the gunmen to protect them against charging cavalry while they reloaded.

Then guns called muskets were invented. They fired more accurately but at first they were too heavy to hold. The musketeers had to use forked sticks to support their guns.

Pistols were less accurate than muskets and fired a shorter distance. They were usually used by cavalry who rode at the enemy, fired at them and rode away to reload.

Towards the end of the 17th century soldiers started to use bayonets (blades which attach to the end of a gun). Gunmen could now defend themselves at close-quarters.

8 Instead of relying on their nobles to raise armies, or hiring mercenary soldiers, kings began to set up permanent armies of their own. These armies were much more highly-trained than before and could obey orders at speed. Commanders had to study hard to learn how to plan their battles and campaigns.

9 War at sea changed too. The Dutch and English developed lighter ships which could turn much more quickly. This helped the English fleet to defeat the Spanish Armada.

10 On ships, cannons were placed along each side. Enemies tried to fire "broadside" at each other so they would have more chance of hitting their target.

11 Disease, bad food and harsh punishments made life at sea very hard. Governments often used "press-gangs" to kidnap men for the navy and take them to sea by force.

Key dates

AD1455/1485 **Wars of the Roses**: civil war in England.

AD1494/1559 **Italian Wars**: Italian states fighting each other. France and the Holy Empire joined in.

AD1524/1525 **Peasants' War** in Germany: the German peasants rebelled.

AD1562/1598 **Wars of Religion in France**: fighting between French Catholics and Protestants.

AD1568/1609 **Dutch Revolt**: the Dutch rebelled against their Spanish rulers.

AD1588 The **Spanish Armada** was defeated by the English fleet.

AD1618/1648 **Thirty Years War**: fought mainly in Germany. Involved most of the countries of Europe.

AD1642/1649 **Civil War** in England.

AD1648/1653 **Wars of the "Fronde"**: two rebellions against the French government.

AD1652/1654, **Wars between the Dutch and**
1665/1667 & **the English.** Fought at sea.
1672/1674 Caused by rivalry over trade.

AD1701/1714 **War of the Spanish Succession**: France and Spain against England, Austria and Holland.

AD1733/1735 **War of the Polish Succession**: Austria and Russia against France and Spain about who should rule Poland.

AD1740/1748 **War of the Austrian Succession**: Austria, Britain and Russia against France and Prussia.

The Incas

The Incas lived in the mountains of Peru in South America. Their capital was a city called Cuzco. From about 1440 onwards they began to conquer neighbouring lands and build up a huge empire. The empire lasted about a hundred years before Spanish soldiers arrived in search of gold and conquered them.

White llamas to be sacrificed.

Temple

Atahualpa

Body of Huayna Capac

Musicians with drums, rattles and flutes.

The emperor of the Incas was called the Inca. His people thought he was descended from the Sun and when he died his body was preserved and treated with great honour.

This is the funeral procession of an emperor called Huayna Capac. His son, Atahualpa, became the new emperor by fighting his half-brother, Huascar.

Unfortunately this war, was just before the Spaniards arrived and it greatly weakened the Incas in their fight against the European invaders.

Inca priests were very important people. They held services, heard confessions and foretold the future by looking into the fire. The Sun was their chief god.

Women were taught how to weave and spin wool. Some women, who were specially chosen for their beauty, became priestesses called the Virgins of the Sun.

The Incas were very skilled at making things out of gold. This gold glove was found in a tomb. Beside it is a model of a god, set with precious stones.

A farming village

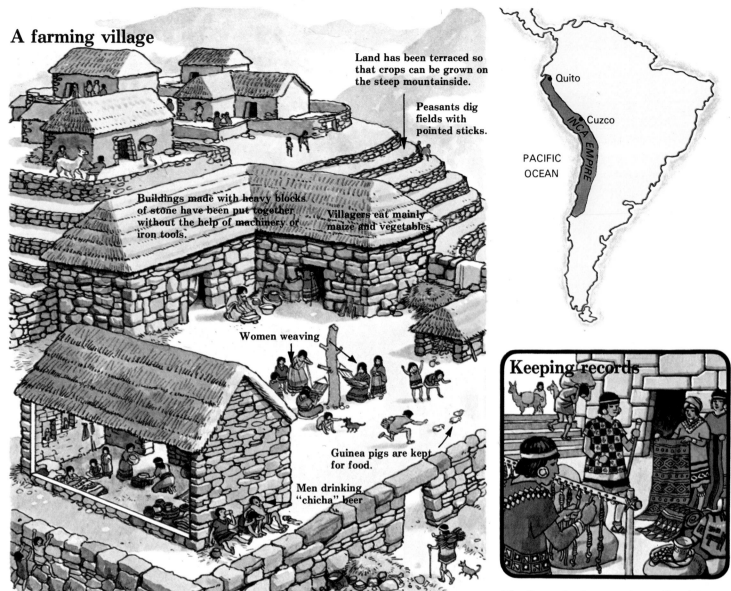

Land has been terraced so that crops can be grown on the steep mountainside.

Peasants dig fields with pointed sticks.

Buildings made with heavy blocks of stone have been put together without the help of machinery or iron tools.

Villagers eat mainly maize and vegetables

Women weaving

Guinea pigs are kept for food.

Men drinking "chicha" beer

Quito

Cuzco

PACIFIC OCEAN

INCA EMPIRE

All the land belonged to the Inca. One third of the crops was kept by peasants, who lived in mountain villages, like this one, and worked on the land. Another third went to the priests and the last third went to the Inca. With his share he paid his officials, soldiers and craftsmen.

Keeping records

The Incas had no system of writing but their officials used "quipus" to help them record things. Coloured strings stood for objects. Knots tied in the strings stood for numbers.

Roads and messengers

A well-maintained network of roads linked all parts of the huge Inca empire. There were hanging bridges, made of twisted straw and vines, across the mountain chasms. These roads and bridges were built and repaired by peasants sent from their villages to serve the emperor. There were no wheeled vehicles so goods were carried by llamas and relays of fast runners carried messages and quipus across the empire. There were rest houses, a day's journey apart, for people on official business to stay in.

The Discovery of America

Until the end of the 15th century, Europeans did not know that the huge continent of America existed. Explorers and traders had made long and difficult journeys eastwards to China and India, bringing back spices, silks and jewels. These were in such demand in Europe that people thought there might be a quicker way to the Far East by sea. The Portuguese sailed to the east round Africa, but others thought it might be quicker to go westwards. When they did, they found America in the way.

1

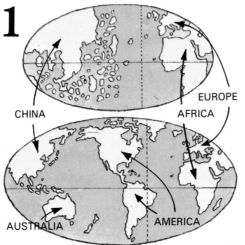

These two maps show the world as people in Europe thought it looked in about 1490 (top) and as it really looked (bottom).

2

An Italian, called Christopher Columbus, persuaded King Ferdinand and Queen Isabella of Spain to pay for an expedition to find China by sailing west instead of east. He set off in 1492 with three ships.

1 The Spanish conquerors

1 Spanish adventurers ("conquistadors") started to explore the mainland, hoping to find treasure. They discovered the Aztecs in Mexico and the Incas in Peru.

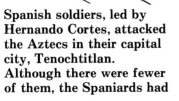

Spanish soldiers, led by Hernando Cortes, attacked the Aztecs in their capital city, Tenochtitlan. Although there were fewer of them, the Spaniards had much better weapons than the Indians, who had never seen horses before. The Spaniards soon conquered the whole of Mexico and called it New Spain.

2

With the help of his Indian interpreter, Dona Marina, Cortes won the support of several Indian tribes, who helped him to defeat the Aztecs.

3

In Peru, the Spanish, led by Pizarro, captured the Inca emperor. To buy his freedom he filled a room with gold. But he was killed and Peru conquered.

4

The Spanish tried to make all the Indians become Christians. Indians who went on worshipping their own gods were burnt to death.

5

The Spaniards treated the Indians very cruelly. Many were put to work in silver mines. Thousands died of illnesses brought over from Europe.

3

After five weeks, Columbus reached what he thought were islands off China but were, in fact, the West Indies. Later, he made three more voyages and reached the mainland of America.

4

To stop Spain and Portugal fighting about who owned the newly discovered lands, the Pope drew a line on the map. All new lands east of the line went to Portugal, those to the west went to Spain.

5

There were many expeditions to explore the new lands. The first to sail round South America was led by Magellan. He was killed on the way, but his ship returned and was the first to sail right round the world.

Slave trade

The Spanish and Portuguese brought ships full of Africans over to work as slaves. They tried to stop other countries joining in this trade, but some captains, like the Englishman John Hawkins, ignored their ban.

Pirates

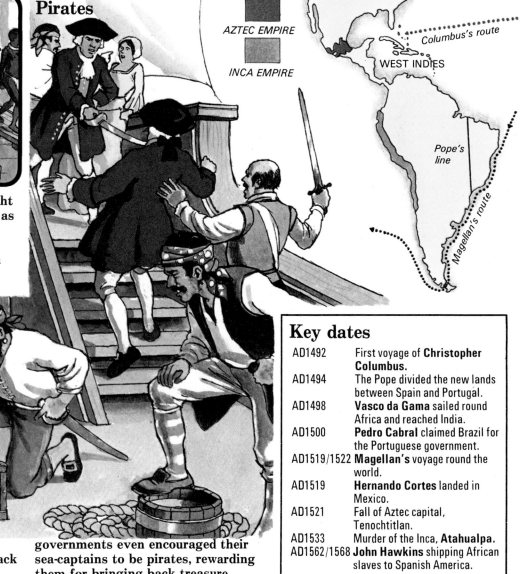

AZTEC EMPIRE

INCA EMPIRE

Columbus's route

WEST INDIES

Pope's line

Magellan's route

Spanish treasure ships were often attacked by pirates on their way back to Spain. The French and English governments even encouraged their sea-captains to be pirates, rewarding them for bringing back treasure.

Key dates

AD1492	First voyage of **Christopher Columbus.**
AD1494	The Pope divided the new lands between Spain and Portugal.
AD1498	**Vasco da Gama** sailed round Africa and reached India.
AD1500	**Pedro Cabral** claimed Brazil for the Portuguese government.
AD1519/1522	**Magellan's** voyage round the world.
AD1519	**Hernando Cortes** landed in Mexico.
AD1521	Fall of Aztec capital, Tenochtitlan.
AD1533	Murder of the Inca, **Atahualpa.**
AD1562/1568	**John Hawkins** shipping African slaves to Spanish America.

Muslim Empires

From about 1300, a Muslim people called the Ottoman Turks began to build up an empire. In 1453 they captured Constantinople, the centre of the Orthodox Christian Church, and renamed the city Istanbul. Its great cathedral, St Sophia, shown here, became a mosque.

The Ottomans wanted to conquer Europe. Led by Sultan, Suleiman the Magnificent, they defeated the Hungarian army at the Battle of Mohács, and took control of Hungary. They continued to threaten Europe until 1683, when they besieged Vienna and were heavily defeated.

The Sultan's palace

Slaves

This is a slave. The Ottomans chose boys from the Christian areas of their empire, took them away from their families and brought them up as Muslims.

Most of the boys were trained to be soldiers called Janissaries. They were the best troops in the Ottomans' army.

The cleverest of these boys were given a good education, and later they were made government officials.

The Ottoman Sultans spent much of their time in the Topkapi Saray, their splendid palace in Istanbul. Here the Sultan is receiving an envoy from Europe. European princes were eager to buy Turkish goods and make alliances with the Turks.

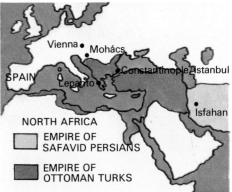

Vienna • Mohács

SPAIN Lepanto Constantinople Istanbul

Isfahan

NORTH AFRICA

EMPIRE OF SAFAVID PERSIANS

EMPIRE OF OTTOMAN TURKS

Muslims in Persia

1

The Persians, like the Ottomans, were Muslims, but they belonged to a different group of Muslims, called the Shi'ites. This mosque is in Isfahan, their capital city.

2

The Persians and Ottomans often fought each other over religion and land. Their wars lasted on and off for over 200 years.

3

The royal family of Persia was called the Safavids. During the reign of their greatest shah (king), Abbas I, the luxuries of Persia became famous throughout the world.

Spain and the Muslims

1

Muslims had overrun Spain in the 8th century. They were finally driven out when King Ferdinand and Queen Isabella conquered Granada, the last Muslim kingdom in Spain.

2

Some Muslims stayed on in Spain and became Christians. But the Spaniards never trusted them and years later their descendants were banished.

3

The Spanish wanted to keep the Ottomans out of the Mediterranean Sea. In 1571, they defeated them in the great Battle of Lepanto.

4

Fierce pirates from North Africa raided the coasts of Spain and other European countries and carried off people to sell as slaves in Muslim lands.

The Habsburgs

SPANISH HABSBURG LANDS

AUSTRIAN HABSBURG LANDS

The Habsburgs were the most powerful ruling family in Europe in the 16th century. They were the rulers of Austria and most of Central Europe and in 1516 the Habsburg Archduke, Charles V, inherited Spain and the newly won Spanish territories in America too. When Charles died, his empire was divided between his son, Philip II of Spain, and his brother Ferdinand, Archduke of Austria, and from then on Spain and Austria were ruled by separate branches of the Habsburg family.

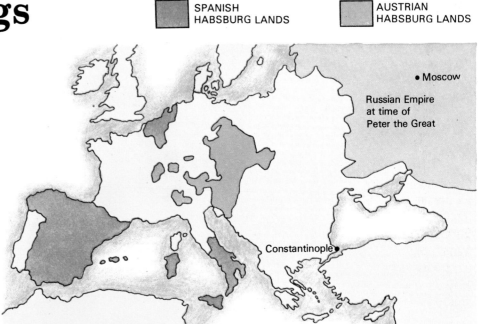

Moscow

Russian Empire at time of Peter the Great

Constantinople

1

Fabulous riches were sent to Spain from South America, but wars against the French, the Protestants and the Turks cost so much that the kings of Spain were always in debt.

2

You can see some of the magnificent clothes worn at the Spanish court in the paintings of Velasquez, King Philip IV's court artist. This is Philip's daughter, Margarita Teresa.

3

The Spanish kings were strong supporters of the Catholic Church. They encouraged the Inquisition to find and punish heretics and declared war on Protestant countries.

4

At this time there were many famous writers and artists in Spain. This is Don Quixote with his servant Sancho Panza, from the book *Don Quixote* written by Miguel de Cervantes.

Holy Roman Emperors

This is the Holy Roman Emperor, who was elected by a group of seven German princes. They always elected the Habsburg Archduke of Austria because the Habsburgs were so powerful. This meant that the

Archduke ruled over the hundreds of different German states. This was a difficult task as many of the German princes had become Protestant and resented having a Catholic ruler.

The Tsars

Before 1450, Russia was divided into several different states, each with its own ruler. During the 15th century, the Grand Prince of Moscow gradually gained control of all the states. The Russians belonged to the Orthodox Christian Church, which had its centre at Constantinople. But when the Turks, who were Muslims, conquered Constantinople in 1453, Moscow saw itself as the centre of the Orthodox Church.

1

Grand Prince Ivan III of Moscow was the first to use the title "Tsar" and have this double-headed eagle as his emblem.

2

Ivan III ordered that Moscow's fortress, the Kremlin, should be rebuilt. He brought in Italian architects who built the cathedral, shown here, inside its walls.

3

4

Ivan IV (1533/1584), often known as Ivan the Terrible because of his cruelty, won great victories over the Tartars and also gained control of all the Russian nobles.

He encouraged trade with Europe and is here receiving envoys from Elizabeth I of England.

When Ivan the Terrible died, the nobles fought for power until a national assembly chose Michael Romanov, shown here, to be the Tsar.

Peter the Great

Tsar Peter the Great (1689-1725) wanted Russia to become a powerful modern state. He forced his nobles to become more European by making them cut their beards off.

Peter went to Holland and England to learn about ship-building. He brought European craftsmen back with him to build him a strong, new navy.

In 1709, Peter led the Russians to a great victory over Sweden, their main rival, at the Battle of Poltava.

Peter wanted Russia to have the grandest capital city in Europe, so he built St Petersburg (now Leningrad) on the edge of the Baltic Sea.

The Elizabethans

From 1485 to 1603, England was ruled by a family called the Tudors. The best-known of the Tudor rulers are Henry VIII, who separated the English Church from the Roman Catholic, and his daughter, Elizabeth I. When Elizabeth was only three, her mother, Anne Boleyn, was executed. During the reigns of her half-brother Edward VI and half-sister Mary, Elizabeth's life was often in danger, but she survived to become one of England's most brilliant rulers.

This is a painting of Elizabeth. She reigned for 45 years, keeping a magnificent court where she inspired writers, artists and explorers. She never married.

This is a Protestant preacher. Elizabeth declared that the Church of England was Protestant, but she did not persecute people who had other beliefs unless they plotted against her.

Explorers

This is Sir Walter Raleigh. He introduced tobacco and potatoes to England from America. He also tried to start a colony in America, but it was unsuccessful.

Some explorers tried to find a way to the Far East by sailing north-west or north-east. They all failed because their ships could not break through the ice.

Once the explorers had discovered new lands and sea-routes, merchants banded together to form companies to trade overseas, licensed by the government.

The Globe theatre

The more expensive seats are in the galleries.

Pit where poorer people and apprentices stand.

The theatre is built of wood with a thatched roof so there is always a danger of fire. (It did, in fact, burn down in 1613.)

Francis Drake

Francis Drake was a great sailor who led daring attacks on Spanish ships and colonies in South America and captured a lot of treasure from them. The Spaniards hated him, but after he had sailed round the world the queen had him knighted on his ship, the Golden Hind. Later, when the Spaniards sent an Armada (fleet) to invade England, Drake played a leading part in their defeat.

Key dates

AD1505/1585 **Thomas Tallis'** life.
AD1540/1623 **William Byrd's** life.
AD1547/1619 **Nicholas Hilliard's** life.
AD1555   Muscovy company given licence to trade with Russia.
AD1563   Elizabethan Church settlement.
AD1564/1616 **William Shakespeare's** life.
AD1577/1580 **Francis Drake** sailed round the world.
AD1584   **Walter Raleigh** set up colony in Virginia.
AD1588   Defeat of Spanish Armada.
AD1597   Globe theatre opened.
AD1600   East India Company given first licence.
AD1601   Poor Law.

By avoiding expensive wars, Elizabeth helped England become very wealthy. The nobles and middle classes spent their money on splendid houses, furniture and clothes.

Beggars and thieves were a terrible problem. A new law was made which said that all districts must provide work for the poor and shelter those who could not work.

Portraits

We know what many famous Elizabethans looked like from the miniature portraits by an artist called Nicholas Hilliard. This is a picture he painted of himself.

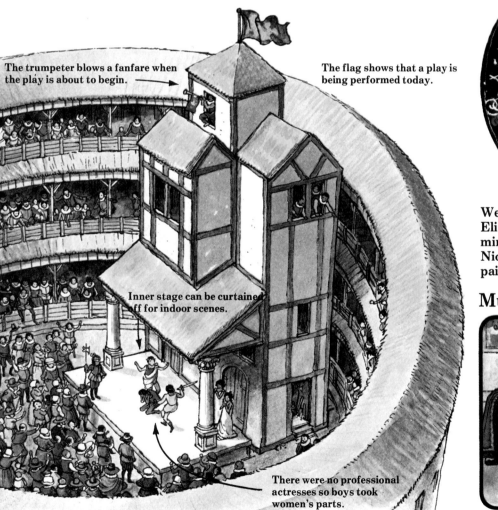

The trumpeter blows a fanfare when the play is about to begin.

The flag shows that a play is being performed today.

Inner stage can be curtained off for indoor scenes.

There were no professional actresses so boys took women's parts.

The Globe in London was the most famous of the theatres built at this time. The first one was opened in 1576. Before this, plays were performed in inn courtyards and town squares.

Shakespeare was an actor and writer with one of the London companies. He wrote at least 36 plays and many of them were first performed at the Globe theatre.

Musicians

Several great musicians lived at this time. Two of the most famous were Thomas Tallis and William Byrd. They composed music to be played at home as well as a great deal of church music.

European Settlers

An Indian village

Land cleared by burning.

Boys fishing

Chief

Long houses made of bark.

Party of hunters bringing a deer home.

Palisade made of tree trunks.

Ritual dance

When the first Europeans arrived in North America, there were hundreds of different tribes of native people there. Each had their own customs, language and way of life. Those on the east coast, where the settlers first landed, were farmers, hunters and food gatherers. They lived in small villages and grew corn and some vegetables. This picture is based on drawings made by some of the early European settlers. The arrival of Europeans in the early 17th century was a disaster for these Indians. Many of them died of diseases brought from Europe and many others were killed or driven from their lands.

Mississippi River

The Appalachian Mountains

New England

Louisiana

• Boston

• Jamestown

13 colonies

In 1607 a group of English settlers set up a colony at Jamestown in Virginia. Here, their leader, Captain John Smith, is being rescued from death by Pocahontas, the daughter of the local Indian chief.

Another group of English people, who became known as the Pilgrim Fathers, sailed to America in 1620 in the ship, "Mayflower". They were Puritans, who wanted freedom to worship God in their own way.

5

The Puritans called the area where they settled New England. During their first winter they had a terrible struggle getting enough food.

Local Indians helped the English to survive. After their first harvest they held a feast to thank God. "Thanksgiving Day" is still celebrated in America.

Many other Europeans sailed with their families and belongings to live in America. Here is a ship full of settlers unloading. Some of them went because they wanted religious freedom, some were escaping from troubles at home and others came in the hope of finding adventure, or a better life and land of their own. The settlers on the east coast soon formed 13 colonies, each with their own laws and system of government. Gradually they were all brought under the control of the British government.

Most colonists settled down as farmers, at first. It was hard work clearing the land, growing crops and defending themselves against hostile Indians.

In the south the colonists started growing tobacco. There was a craze for it in Europe so they grew rich by making African slaves work for them.

Trade with Europe became profitable and some of the money was used to build towns. This is part of 18th century Boston.

A few people, mainly Frenchmen, chose to live as trappers and hunters. They explored along the Mississippi River, claiming land for France.

Plantations and Trading Forts

1 West Indies

Plantation owner

Sugar cane

Overseer

From the 1620s onwards, most of the islands known as the West Indies were taken over by the French and English. They set up sugar plantations and imported African slaves to work on them.

2

Fierce pirates infested the Caribbean Sea at this time. One English pirate called Henry Morgan was eventually knighted by King Charles II.

Key dates

AD1497	**John Cabot** discovered Newfoundland.
AD1523	French begin to explore Canada.
AD1607	English colony set up in Virginia.
AD1608	French founded the settlement of Quebec.
AD1612	First English colony in West Indies set up on Bermuda.
AD1620	The Pilgrim Fathers sailed to America in the Mayflower.
AD1655	English captured Jamaica from Spaniards.
AD1682	The French set up settlements in Louisiana.
AD1759	**General James Wolfe** captured Quebec from the French.
AD1763	Treaty of Paris. England took over Canada from French.

Canadian trading fort

Many French and English people settled in Canada. Some of them were farmers but many of them made a living by trapping animals for fur and catching and salting fish, especially cod. The trappers sold their catch and bought supplies at forts set up by trading companies. The fish and furs were then sent to Europe where they were in great demand.

BRITISH

SPANISH

FRENCH

Hudson's Bay Company

Quebec

CANADA

WEST INDIES

JAMAICA

CARIBBEAN SEA

The capture of Quebec

The lands belonging to England's Hudson Bay Company in Canada and the 13 colonies in America were separated by the French colonies in Canada. From the 1680s onwards, rivalry between the French and British grew and fighting broke out. Here British troops, led by general Wolfe, are reaching the top of the very steep cliffs above the St Lawrence River before making a surprise attack on the French city of Quebec. After the capture of Quebec, the English went on to gain control of the whole of Canada.

The Kingdom of Benin

1

Today Benin is a small town in Nigeria, but between AD1450 and AD1850 it was the capital city of a great kingdom. European explorers brought back reports that Benin's warriors were highly disciplined and very brave, and were constantly fighting to win more land and slaves.

2

The people of Benin had no system of writing, but they made bronze plaques to record important events. This plaque shows their king, who was called the Oba, sacrificing a cow. The Obas spent most of their time in religious ceremonies and let their counsellors govern.

3

The Portuguese were the first Europeans to explore the coast of Africa. Soon others came, eager to buy ivory, gold and especially slaves sold by the local chiefs.

4

The most promising boys were trained as hunters. If they were very good they could become elephant hunters, armed with blow-guns and poisonous darts.

5

Benin lost its power in the 19th century, but the people still survive. This present-day chief is dressed for a festival in honour of the Oba's father.

Music

This carving shows a drummer playing at a ceremony at the Oba's court. The musicians of Benin also played bells and elephant-tusk trumpets.

Carvings

The people of Benin made beautiful portrait heads, like this one of a queen mother. It was the queen mother's duty to bring up the Oba's heir.

There were many skilled craftsmen in Benin. Besides bronze plaques and portrait heads, they made lovely things from ivory, like the bracelets, shown above.

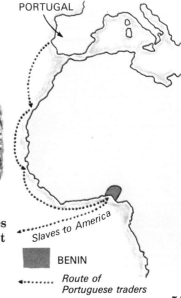

PORTUGAL

Slaves to America

BENIN

Route of Portuguese traders

The Mogul Empire

Muslim warriors had been invading and setting up kingdoms in India since before the 10th century. The most famous Muslim invaders were the Moguls, who were descended from the Mongols. In 1526, they founded the great Mogul Empire in north-west India which lasted until 1858. During their rule, great progress was made in the arts and sciences. Most Indians continued to work on the land, however, as their ancestors had done for centuries before them.

This is the first Mogul emperor, Babur (1526-1530). He was a descendent of the Mongol chiefs, Tamerlane and Genghis Khan.

This is the court of Babur's grandson, Akbar (1556-1605), greatest of the Mogul emperors. He was a good soldier and a wise ruler. He encouraged artists and brought scholars of all religions together to try to find one religion.

The Moguls were strongly influenced by Persian art and learning. This is Akbar's son, whose wife was Persian. Her name, Nurjahan, meant "Light of the World".

Many wonderful buildings were put up by the Moguls. The most famous is the Taj Mahal. It was built by Emperor Shah Jahan, as a tomb for his wife Mumtaz Mahal.

The Mogul emperors and nobles enjoyed hunting. Sometimes they used cheetahs for hunting gazelle. They also hunted tigers while riding on the backs of elephants.

European merchants came to India to buy silks, cotton, ivory, dyes and spices. Gradually they set up trading posts throughout India.

As the power of the Mogul rulers grew weaker, the British and French used the rivalry of lesser princes to increase their own power. Here, one of the princes is preparing for battle.

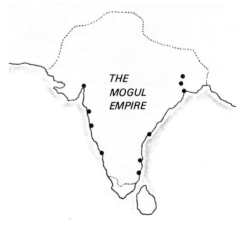

THE MOGUL EMPIRE

• BRITISH AND FRENCH TRADING POSTS

Ming and Ch'ing Emperors

The emperors of China lived in Peking, in a fantastic palace called the "Forbidden City". Here they were surrounded by richly decorated buildings and lovely gardens. The

Ming dynasty (family line) of emperors (AD1368/1644) cut themselves off from the government and let their officials rule for them. In AD1644 the last Ming emperor

committed suicide and the Ch'ing dynasty won power. They ruled until AD1911. Many of the Ch'ing emperors were clever rulers and brought peace and prosperity to China.

1

This figure, carved in ivory, represents a public official. To obtain this job he had to take a series of very difficult exams.

2

Chinese doctors knew how to prepare medicines by boiling up herbs. They also treated patients by sticking needles in them (acupuncture).

3

Here is a scene from *The Water Margin*. This was one of China's few novels. It tells a story about bandits who protected the poor against wicked officials.

4

European missionaries, like these Jesuit priests were, at first, welcomed by the emperors, but later they were driven out.

5

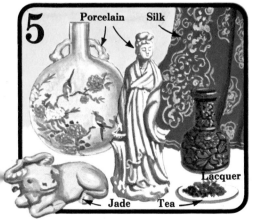

Porcelain   Silk

Lacquer

Jade   Tea

Many people in Europe wanted to buy beautifully-made Chinese goods, like these. But Europeans had to pay in gold and silver because China did not want European goods.

Farming

In the countryside life continued with few changes. New crops, such as maize, were introduced from America by Spanish and Portuguese traders. During the period of peace under the

Ch'ing emperors the population began to increase. At first this did not matter, but later, it became difficult to grow enough grain to feed everyone.

Life in Japan

The emperors of Japan were greatly honoured, but had no real power. The country was ruled by an official called the Shogun. The first Europeans reached Japan in the 1540s and for nearly a century they traded with the Japanese. But then the Shogun expelled all foreign merchants, except the Chinese and the Dutch, and the Japanese people remained totally cut off from the rest of the world until 1854.

In 1467, civil war broke out. For over 100 years, the local barons, called daimyos, fought each other. They built huge castles like this one, half-fortress, half-palace, where they lived with their warriors, the samurai. The samurai believed that the only honourable way of life was to fight for and give loyal service to their daimyo. Eventually, a powerful daimyo called Tokugawa Ieyasu, succeeded in uniting Japan. He became Shogun and ruled from his capital in Edo (now Tokyo). The Tokugawa family held power until 1868.

1

The ancient Japanese Shinto faith became popular again in the 18th century. Here a new baby is being brought to a Shinto shrine.

2

Tea drinking developed into an elaborate ceremony, which still plays an important part in Japanese life. Both the ceremony and the tea were originally brought from China by Buddhist monks. The way in which the tea is prepared, served and drunk follows strict rules.

3

Christianity was brought to Japan by Jesuits. They converted many people but later the Shoguns banned Christianity and had many Christians executed.

4

Arranging flowers was a special art, called Ikebana, which at first only men were allowed to do. The type of flowers and the way they are arranged have special meanings.

5

Pictures made by printing from carved blocks of wood became popular at this time. Most of them illustrate the lives of ordinary people.

6

This is a street bookseller in the early 18th century. Poetry and novels were still popular but there were no longer many women writers as there had been earlier.

7

Puppet theatres and a type of musical play called "Kabuki" became very popular. These were livelier and more realistic than older Japanese dramas.

A Dutch island

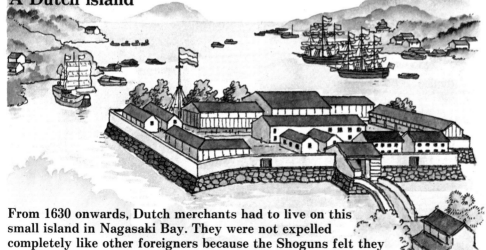

From 1630 onwards, Dutch merchants had to live on this small island in Nagasaki Bay. They were not expelled completely like other foreigners because the Shoguns felt they would not try to conquer or convert the Japanese. A bridge linked the island to the land, but the Dutch were not allowed to cross it.

Key dates

AD1467/1568	Period of civil war in Japan.
AD1543	First Portuguese traders reached Japan. Other Europeans follow.
AD1549/1551	**St Francis Xavier** working in Japan.
AD1592 & 1597	Japanese invaded Korea.
AD1600/1868	Tokugawa family rule.
AD1603	**Tokugawa Ieyasu** became Shogun.
AD1606/1630	Christians persecuted.
AD1623/1639	All Europeans, except a few Dutch, left Japan.

Merchants and Trade

Once explorers had discovered new lands and sea-routes in the 16th century, there was a huge increase in trade between Europe and the rest of the world. By the 17th century the main trading countries were Holland, England and France. In these countries the merchants and middle classes who organized this trade became very wealthy and began to copy the life-style of the nobles. Even some of the ordinary working people benefited from this increase in wealth.

Groups of merchants, like these, set up trading companies in which people could buy shares. The shareholders' money was used to pay the cost of trading ventures and any profit was divided amongst the shareholders.

Many merchants bought goods from people who worked in their own homes and sold them abroad. Here a merchant's agent is buying cloth from a family workshop.

Companies hired ships to export their goods. Countries competing for overseas trade had to have good ships, sailors and ports. Dutch ships were among the best in Europe.

Rich merchants began to band together to set up banks to lend money. For this service they charged a fee called "interest". People could also bring their money to the bank for safe-keeping. The first bankers were Italian merchants. In the 17th century London and Amsterdam became the most important banking cities.

In some of the big cities of Europe, coffee houses became the places where people met to buy and sell shares and discuss business.

It soon became more convenient to have a proper building for use as a market where people could buy and sell shares. This is the Amsterdam Stock Exchange, built in 1613. Soon there were stock exchanges like this in all the important trading centres of Europe.

Special insurance companies were set up. Merchants paid them a fee and if their trading expeditions met with disaster the insurance company stood the cost.

1 The new middle classes

As the merchant classes grew richer, they built themselves big town houses. The fashionable areas of big cities had pavements and wide streets.

2

The new middle classes wanted to live like the nobles. Many of them became rich enough to buy country estates and obtained titles. Some of the nobility looked down on them but others were happy to marry into these wealthy families.

3

Governments needed to understand business and finance so sometimes men from the merchant classes were chosen as royal ministers and advisers.

4

We know what many of the Dutch merchants of this time looked like because many of them paid artists to paint their portraits.

5

Many of the paintings of this time, especially Dutch ones, show us how merchant families lived and what their homes looked like.

6

In every country there were still many desperately poor people. Some nobles and merchants tried to help the poor. They founded hospitals, homes for old people and orphanages. Here a group of merchants' wives are inspecting an orphanage run by nuns.

Dutch merchants find Australia

On their trips to the east, Dutch sailors discovered Australia, which they called New Holland. Some people were wrecked there and tried to set up settlements but all their early attempts failed.

The Dutch controlled most of the important spice trade between Europe and the East Indies. This made Holland the greatest trading nation in Europe for much of the 17th century. This map shows the Dutch empire in the East Indies and the things they went there to buy.

- Dutch bases
- △ Rice
- ■ Pepper
- ○ Sugar
- ▲ Cloves
- □ Nutmeg
- ◊ Ivory
- ● Diamonds
- ▲ Tin
- Precious woods

EAST INDIES

AUSTRALIA

Kings and Parliaments

In the 17th and 18th centuries much of Europe was ruled by kings, queens and emperors who were extremely powerful. These rulers are known as "absolute monarchs". The court of

Louis XIV of France was the most brilliant in Europe. This is the Hall of Mirrors in his palace at Versailles. Louis encouraged the French nobles to come and live at his court, and

spend their time in a round of entertainments, so that he could keep an eye on them. Other monarchs built themselves great palaces too and tried to imitate Louis' way of life.

1 The English parliament

1

Parliament supporter ("roundhead")

King's supporter ("cavalier")

King Charles I of England tried to ignore parliament and rule like an absolute monarch. Many people were so unhappy with the way he ruled that in 1642 civil war broke out.

2

The king was defeated and executed. Oliver Cromwell, the leader of the parliamentarian army became ruler. He could not get parliament to agree with him so he too tried to rule without parliament.

3

Oliver Cromwell died in 1658. His son was incompetent and no one would support his government. Eventually Charles I's son was invited back and crowned King Charles II.

Parliaments hardly ever met. The king took all the important decisions. His ministers could only advise him and carry out his instructions. In order to keep control a successful ruler, like Louis XIV, had to spend hours every day with his ministers in meetings like this one.

Sometimes the king's favourites became very powerful. Louis XV let Madame du Pompadour, shown above, make important decisions.

The king made the laws and could put his enemies in prison if he wanted. Law-courts did what the king wanted.

Absolute monarchs usually kept large, permanent armies. Frederick the Great of Prussia, which is now part of Germany, was a brilliant military commander. Here he is inspecting his troops.

Monarchs often brought great painters, musicians and writers to their courts. As a child, Mozart played the piano at the court of Maria Teresa.

To add to the strength of their countries rulers set up industries. Some of these produced luxury goods such as tapestries, silk and glass. This is a glassworks.

Parliament's power increased, however, and the king's minister had to have the support of its members. This is Robert Walpole one of the most successful ministers of the 18th century.

Members of parliament formed two political parties called the Whigs and the Tories. Only people who owned property worth more than a certain value could vote.

Key dates

AD1642	English Civil War began.
AD1643/1715	**Louis XIV** ruled France.
AD1649	**Charles I** was executed.
AD1658	**Oliver Cromwell** died.
AD1660/1685	Reign of **Charles II**.
AD1682/1725	**Peter the Great** ruled Russia.
AD1715/1774	**Louis XV** ruled France.
AD1730/1741	**Robert Walpole** was Prime Minister.
AD1740/1780	**Maria Teresa** ruled Austria.
AD1740/1786	**Frederick the Great** ruled Prussia (now part of Germany).
AD1756/1791	Life of **Mozart**.
AD1762/1796	**Catherine the Great** ruled Russia.

Sports and Pastimes

In the 16th century, nobles and kings played an early version of tennis on special courts. Bowls were also a favourite game at this time.

A cruel but popular sport was cock-fighting. Cocks were specially trained to fight, often to the death. The crowd placed bets on which bird would win.

Fox-hunting was a sport for the wealthy. Horse-racing, which was introduced later on, interested a wider audience.

All classes of people liked to watch bear or bull baiting. The animal was put in a ring and fierce dogs set onto it to kill it. Often some of the dogs got killed as well.

The English village of Hambledon had the first recognized cricket club. The game was later introduced to many of the countries in the British Empire.

Special gambling houses were set up where people could gamble on cards and dice. Huge sums of money would change hands every evening.

Fencing and shooting were sports, but gentlemen sometimes killed each other in duels with swords or pistols, fought over an insult or gambling quarrel.

Boxing grew in popularity, particularly in the early years of the 19th century. Many young noblemen learned to box, but did not fight in public contests.

In the late 18th century, sea-bathing became fashionable for people who could afford to travel to the coast.

They used "bathing machines" to stop people watching them from the beach.

Pirates, Highwaymen and Smugglers

During the 18th century traders and explorers on long sea trips were likely to be attacked by bands of pirates, who sailed the seas looking for ships to plunder. The West Indies, where many pirates hid among the islands, was an especially dangerous area.

Travel by land was slow, uncomfortable and dangerous. The roads were not made up and coaches sometimes overturned. There were highwaymen too, who held up the coaches and demanded the passengers' money and valuables.

European countries charged taxes, called customs duties, on goods brought into the country. To avoid paying the taxes, smugglers worked secretly, often at night, bringing brandy, silks and other expensive goods from ships moored off the shore.

Towns and villages along the coast had Coast Guards and Excise Officers whose job it was to look out for smugglers. Once onshore the goods had to be hidden until they could be sold. You can still see old inns with secret cellars where smuggled goods were hidden.

When countries such as Britain and France were at war, trade between them was supposed to stop, but the smugglers went on carrying the goods and made great profits. If they were caught they were severely punished and sometimes even hung.

A Revolution in Farming

In the 18th century farming methods in England changed completely. The experiments of a few enthusiastic landowners led to the invention of new tools, the introduction of new crops and new ways of improving the soil and breeding better animals. Landowners found it easier to introduce improvements if they gave each farmer a block of land, instead of thin strips in different fields as was usual then. These changes, known as the "Agricultural Revolution", later happened in other parts of Europe.

By using only their best animals for breeding, farmers produce much bigger, healthier animals.

New crops, like turnips and clover are stored in barns, so animals can now be kept and fed over the winter instead of being killed.

Most villagers cannot produce enough food for themselves, now that the common land has been divided up. They have sold their land and now work for other farmers for wages.

Clergyman's house

Village inn

Hedges have been planted round the fields.

The village green is all that is left of the old common (land which could be used by all the villagers), which has been shared out as farmland.

The landowner built these cottages for villagers who work for him.

Vegetable plot

On pages 8 and 9, you can see what this village looked like in the Middle Ages.

66

Village windmill for grinding corn.

House of chief landowner of the village, often called the squire. Some other villagers own their land, but he still owns the most.

New plough cuts deeper furrows.

Seed drill sows seeds in straight lines.

This carrier has just delivered some goods to the house.

Doctor's house

Animal manure is spread on the land to make it more fertile.

Ditch for draining land that used to be too wet for growing crops.

Landowner (squire)

Blacksmith

This farmer owns the land he farms.

Village shop

This family is leaving to go and work in a town.

Milkmaid

Woman spinning

Hoeing keeps the crop free of weeds so there will be a bigger harvest.

Landowner's wife

This man rents a farm from the landowner

In this field the farmer grows wheat one year, turnips the next, barley the third year and clover the fourth. This order of growing crops keeps the field fertile. Fields are no longer left unplanted every third year.

Machines and Factories

In the first half of the 18th century, most people in Britain still lived and worked in the countryside. Woollen and cotton cloth, produced in the north of England, were the chief manufactured goods. Before 1750 cloth was mainly made by hand, in people's homes. But by 1850 it was being made by machines in factories. The new factories employed lots of people and towns quickly grew up round them. These changes in working life have become known as the "Industrial Revolution".

1 Making cloth

Spinning · Weaving · Combing wool ready for spinning.

Britain produced a great deal of woollen cloth. In the first half of the 18th century, most of it was made by villagers in their homes and sold to visiting merchants.

2

Then machines like this were invented. They helped spinners and weavers to work much faster. Later they were adapted to be driven by water, and later still by steam.

Steam power

This is one of Watt's steam engines.

The early factories used water power to make their machines go. Various people experimented with the idea of using steam. Eventually a Scotsman called James Watt found out how to make steam engines drive the wheels of other machines and these were soon being used in factories.

Iron

This is an iron works. Iron was needed for making the new machines, but iron-smelting needed charcoal and the wood for making this was in short supply.

Coal was no good as its fumes made the iron brittle. Then, Abraham Darby discovered coal could be turned into coke which was pure enough for making iron.

1 Coal

People had been using coal to heat their homes for a long time, but it had been dug only from shallow mines. Deep mines were too dangerous.

2

Safety lamp

Several inventions made mining safer. The safety lamp cut down the danger of explosions. Steam pumps helped prevent flooding and there was also a machine which sucked out stale air.

3

Underground rails made it easier to haul coal to the surface from great depths, but conditions in the mines were still very bad. Small children were used to pull the heavy trucks.

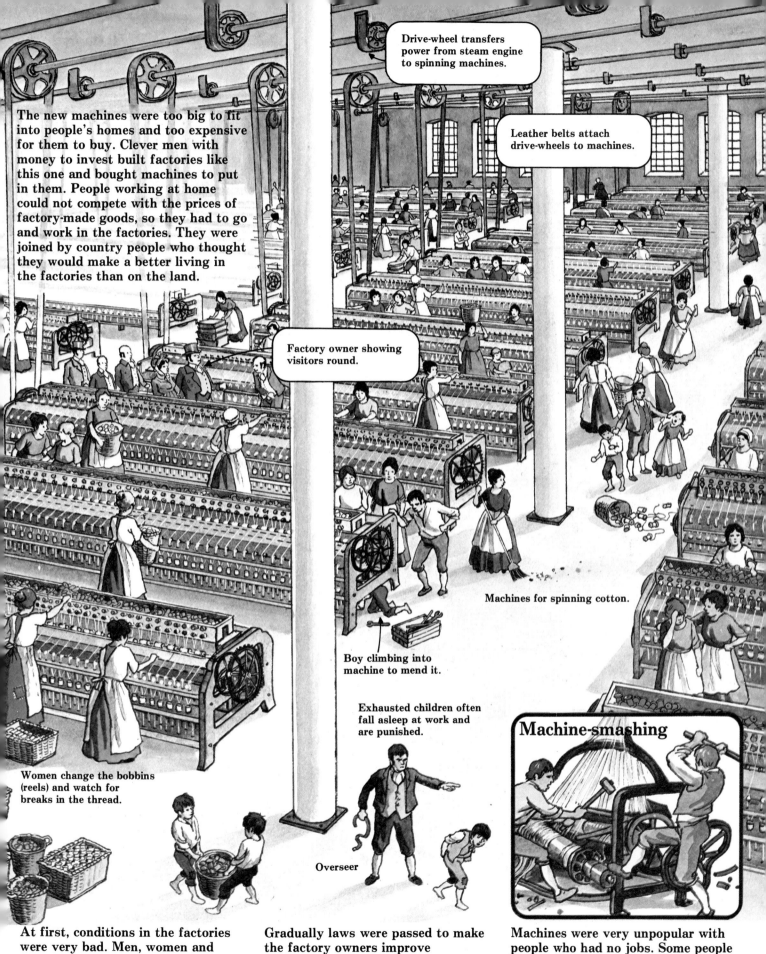

The new machines were too big to fit into people's homes and too expensive for them to buy. Clever men with money to invest built factories like this one and bought machines to put in them. People working at home could not compete with the prices of factory-made goods, so they had to go and work in the factories. They were joined by country people who thought they would make a better living in the factories than on the land.

Drive-wheel transfers power from steam engine to spinning machines.

Leather belts attach drive-wheels to machines.

Factory owner showing visitors round.

Machines for spinning cotton.

Boy climbing into machine to mend it.

Exhausted children often fall asleep at work and are punished.

Women change the bobbins (reels) and watch for breaks in the thread.

Overseer

Machine-smashing

At first, conditions in the factories were very bad. Men, women and children worked very long hours for low wages. Machines had no safety guards and there were bad accidents.

Gradually laws were passed to make the factory owners improve conditions in the factories, make working hours shorter and protect the rights of working people.

Machines were very unpopular with people who had no jobs. Some people even banded together to smash them. One group was called the Luddites after their leader, Ned Ludd.

Life in the New Towns

Where factories were built, new towns quickly grew up to house the factory workers. They were overcrowded and unhealthy places and they caused many problems.

Factory owner's house

Factories

Railway (goods line)

Chimney sweep and apprentice

Policeman

Barrel organ

Hansom cab

Gas lamp

Fruit-seller

Pickpocket

Cheap houses, built back-to-back, were put up for the factory workers, especially in the northern towns. Often there were no toilets or running water. The streets were dirty and the air and rivers polluted by factories.

Diseases spread quickly. Until cheap ways of travelling were developed the workers had to live near the factories, which were often built near coal mines and ironworks.

70

1 The changes in farming and industry left some people without jobs and desperately poor. To get help they had to go and live in "workhouses". Conditions in the workhouses were very harsh to discourage lazy people from using them. Men and women lived in separate quarters so families were split up. Poor people often preferred to live on the streets.

Key dates

AD1733/1793	Invention of several machines for spinning and weaving cloth.
AD1769	**James Watt** invented his first steam engine.
AD1812	Outbreaks of machine-smashing by the Luddites.
AD1824 & 1825	Trade Unions made legal, but with many restrictions.
AD1833	First of many laws passed to improve working conditions in factories.
AD1833, 1870, 1880, 1891, 1902	Education Acts*.
AD1845/1905	Life of **Dr Barnado**.
AD1848	First Public Health Act.
AD1875	First Housing Act.
AD1878	Salvation Army founded.
AD1900	Labour Party founded.
AD1909	Old-age pension Act.
AD1911	National Insurance Act.

An Act is a law passed by parliament.

2 Several reformers tried to help poor people. Dr Barnardo, shown here, set up children's homes and General Booth started a Christian organization called the Salvation Army.

3 Many laws were passed during the 19th century to improve people's lives by cleaning up towns, building better houses and setting up schools where all children could go without paying.

4 Old-age pensions started in 1909. These people are collecting theirs from the post office. In 1911, a law was passed which insured people against sickness and unemployment.

5 Workers began to join together to form trade unions so that they could bargain for better wages and working conditions by threatening to strike. At first the trade unions were illegal but gradually laws were passed which made them legal and gave them the right to picket (stand outside their work places and try to persuade other workers not to go in).

6 Some trade unionists and people who agreed with them formed the Labour Party. In the general election of 1906, 29 of their members were elected to parliament.

Transport and Travel

The Industrial Revolution brought about immense changes in transport and travel. Some important developments happened first in Britain, others happened first in America and other parts of Europe.

In England, companies called Turnpike Trusts were set up. They built and repaired roads and charged people tolls for using them. This is one of the tollgates. Engineers, like Telford and Macadam, found ways of building roads with hard surfaces.

New bridges were also built, many of them iron. This is the Clifton Suspension Bridge in England, designed by Brunel, a famous engineer.

Bicycles were in general use by the 1880s. The early "penny-farthings" were ridden by men, but later models were suitable for women to ride too.

As the population increased during the 19th century, cities grew in size. People had to live further from their work and horse-drawn buses were introduced to provide them with transport. Before long, city streets became packed with traffic.

The first motor cars were made in Germany in 1885. They remained too expensive for anyone but the very wealthy until the 1920s.

1 Canals

In the 18th century, it was much cheaper to send heavy goods by water than by road. Where there were no suitable rivers, canals were cut to link important ports and cities. Locks, like the ones shown here, took the boats up and down slopes. The barges were pulled by horses walking along the "towpath."

In 1869 the Suez Canal, which links the Mediterranean Sea to the Red Sea, was opened. This canal cut several weeks off the journey from Europe to India. Later, in 1915, another long ship canal was opened. This was the Panama Canal in Central America which joined the Atlantic and Pacific Oceans.

Railways

Early type of locomotive designed by famous railway engineer George Stephenson.

The first steam locomotive to run on rails was built in England in 1804 by Richard Trevithick. Twenty years later, the first passenger railway was opened and from then on railways became very popular. They were a quick, cheap and safe way of carrying people and goods. As train services improved, it became possible for ordinary people to go on seaside and country holidays. England's roads and canals were neglected.

London got its first long stretch of underground railway in 1863. Until 1890, when electric trains came in, the underground trains were steam-powered. The tunnels are still filled with the soot they made.

1 Sea travel

Very fast sailing ships called "clippers" were built during the 19th century and used to carry light cargoes such as tea. A completely new kind of ship was also being developed at this time. These ships were built of iron and had steam-engines. They gradually replaced sailing ships.

2 Many lighthouses were built and a life-boat service introduced, making sea travel much safer than it had been in the past.

3 Faster and safer sea travel tempted wealthy people to take holidays abroad. In 1869, Thomas Cook ran his first holiday tour to Egypt.

1 The first flights

The French Montgolfier brothers were the first people to take off into the air. This was in 1783 in a hot-air balloon. Other balloonists tried using hydrogen.

2 At the beginning of the 20th century, two Americans, the Wright brothers, built a glider like this one. Later they built an aeroplane fitted with an engine and in 1903 made the first powered flight.

Key dates

AD1663/1770	Turnpike trusts set up.
AD1783	First ascent of hot air balloon.
AD1804	First steam vehicle to run on rails.
AD1829	First railroads opened in U.S.A.
AD1839	First pedal bicycle made.
AD1863	Opening of first underground railway.
AD1869	Suez Canal opened.
AD1885	**Karl Benz** made a 3-wheeled motor car.
AD1886	**Gottlieb Daimler** made a 4-wheeled motor car.
AD1903	First powered flight.

French Revolution and Napoleon's Wars

1 The King of France, Louis XVI, and his wife, Marie Antoinette, lived in the magnificent palace of Versailles near Paris. Here they were surrounded by rich nobles who hardly paid any taxes. Louis was not a good ruler and they were all unpopular with the people.

2 Many nobles were very arrogant and treated everyone else with scorn. The middle classes were very annoyed by this.

3 The peasants had to pay taxes to the church, the government and their local lord. They also had to work for their lords.

4 By 1789, the government had no more money left, so the king was forced to call a meeting of the States General (parliament), which had not met for 175 years. Later the States General passed many reforms but most people were still not satisfied.

5 On July 14, 1789, a crowd in Paris captured a royal prison called the Bastille. This sparked off riots all over France.

6 The revolution became more violent. The king, queen, nobles and anyone not revolutionary enough were executed by guillotine.

7 European rulers were horrified by events in France and soon the French were at war with most of the rest of Europe. Here a soldier is recruiting people for the French army. Many clever young officers were found, in particular Napoleon Bonaparte.

8 Napoleon was so successful as a military commander that he became First Consul of France and then had himself crowned Emperor.

9 Napoleon gained control of much of Europe. He made his brothers and sisters rulers of the lands he conquered. This map shows the lands ruled by him and members of his family by 1810.

PRUSSIA
AUSTRIA
FRANCE
SPAIN
ITALIAN STATES

10

Napoleon planned to invade Britain, his most determined enemy. But after the British defeated the French at sea in the Battle of Trafalgar, he gave up the idea.

11

In 1812, Napoleon invaded Russia with an army of 600,000 men. He defeated the Tsar's army and marched to Moscow. But the Russians had set fire to Moscow and removed all the provisions. Here the French army is returning home in the middle of winter. Hundreds of thousands of them died from cold and hunger.

12

After his disastrous invasion of Russia, there was a general reaction against Napoleon in Europe. British troops helped the Spanish to drive the French out of Spain.

The Battle of Waterloo

The Battle of Waterloo was the last great battle in the wars against Napoleon. The French were completely defeated by a British army, led by Wellington, and a Prussian army, led by Blücher.

Louis XVIII was made King of France, and Napoleon was imprisoned on the small British island of St Helena in the South Atlantic Ocean, where he died in 1821.

Key dates

AD1789	First meeting of the States General.
AD1792	France went to war with Austria and Prussia.
AD1793/1794	Period called "The Reign of Terror". Hundreds of people guillotined.
AD1804	**Napoleon** became Emperor.
AD1805	Battle of Trafalgar.
AD1808/1814	War between the British and French in Spain and Portugal.
AD1812	**Napoleon's** invasion of Russia.
AD1815	Battle of Waterloo.

New Nations and Ways of Governing

The 18th and 19th centuries were times of great change in the way countries were governed.

There were many revolutions and several new, independent nations emerged.

1 Independence for America

In 1775 war broke out. The British Army were far from home and supplies. The colonists were on their own ground and their riflemen were very good shots.

In 1781 the British surrendered at Yorktown and in 1783 they signed a treaty recognizing the United States of America as an independent nation.

Most European settlers in America lived in the 13 colonies* on the east coast. In the early 18th century Britain helped them in their wars against the Indians and the French. The British then taxed them to pay for the wars. The colonists hated the taxes and sometimes attacked British tax officers.

When the new constitution (set of rules by which a country is governed) had been agreed upon, George Washington was chosen as first President of America.

Key Dates

AD1775/1783	War of American Independence.
AD1789/1797	**George Washington** President of the U.S.A.
AD1818/1883	Life of **Karl Marx**.
AD1859/1860	**General Garibaldi** drove French and Austrians out of Italy.
AD1861	Kingdom of Italy founded.
AD1871	German Empire founded. **William I** became Kaiser and **Bismarck** First Chancellor.

Germany

Early in the 19th century Germany was a group of states, the strongest of which was Prussia. In 1861 William I became King of Prussia. With his chief minister, Bismarck, he gradually brought all Germany under his control. In 1871 William was proclaimed Kaiser (emperor) of Germany.

Battleship being launched

Germany became one of the strongest countries in Europe. It quickly built a large navy, developed its industries and won colonies in Africa and the Far East.

Germans became very interested in their country's history. The operas of Wagner based on tales of German gods and heroes, became very popular.

*A colony is a settlement ruled by the country from which the settlers have come.

Italy

In Italy, some states were independent, some were ruled by France and some by Austria. General Garibaldi and his soldiers, known as the "Red Shirts"(above) helped to drive the foreigners out of Italy and make it an independent nation.

☐ ITALY IN 1866
☐ GERMAN EMPIRE IN 1871

PRUSSIA

1 Ideas about government

In Britain, the people chose which political party should rule by voting at elections. At first few people had the right to vote but gradually it was extended to all men.

2

Some women began to demand the vote. They were called suffragettes.

They held marches and caused as much disturbance as possible to win support.

3

Rulers in many countries were afraid of democracy (people having a say in the running of the country). Soldiers were used against the people who protested.

4

People with revolutionary ideas were sometimes executed or put in prison so they could not lead the people against their ruler.

5

Some people believed any form of government was wrong. They were called anarchists and they killed many political leaders.

6

A German thinker, called Karl Marx, wrote many books with new ideas about government. He wanted people to get rid of their rulers in a revolution and then have new governments run by the working people. Communism is based on his ideas.

Slavery and Civil War

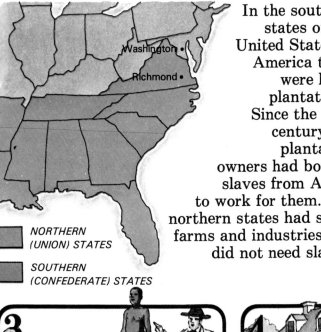

NORTHERN
(UNION) STATES

SOUTHERN
(CONFEDERATE) STATES

In the southern states of the United States of America there were large plantations. Since the 17th century the plantation owners had bought slaves from Africa to work for them. The northern states had small farms and industries and did not need slaves.

The slave trade became well organized. Europeans either captured Africans or bought them from local rulers, like the King of Dahomey, shown here.

Conditions on the ships carrying the slaves to America were dreadful as the more slaves a trader could get on a ship, the greater his profit.

When they reached America, the slaves who had survived the voyage were sold at auctions. They could be sold again at any time and families were often parted.

Some slaves were lucky enough to work in their master's house but most were used as field hands on the plantation. Most estate owners grew either cotton, tobacco or sugar, all

of which need constant attention. Because of the heat African slaves were thought best for this work. Some masters were very cruel but others treated their slaves quite well.

Many slaves tried to escape to the north where they would be free as there was no slavery. A black woman called Harriet Tubman, helped 19 groups of slaves escape.

Protests against slavery began to grow. In 1833 slavery was abolished in the British Empire and the Anti-Slavery Society was founded in America. This is its badge.

In the American Congress (parliament) there were bitter arguments about slavery. The northerners wanted to abolish it but the southerners were determined to keep slaves.

The outbreak of war

In 1861 the southern states elected their own president and broke away from the Union of the United States, declaring themselves a "confederacy" The north thought the states should stay united so war broke out between the Unionists (northerners) and Confederates (southerners). It lasted for four years. There were many fierce battles and nearly 635,000 people lost their lives.

Camp

Mine exploding

Southern (Confederate) flag

Northern (Unionist) flag

Barbed wire

Trench

A new style of fighting developed during the American Civil War. Soldiers made trenches protected by barbed wire. They used mines, hand-grenades and flame throwers.

At first the southerners, led by General Lee, were quite successful. But the north had more soldiers, factories to make weapons and railways to transport them. It used its navy to stop ships bringing supplies to the south. Despite terrible suffering the southerners fought bravely on, but in 1865 they were finally forced to surrender.

1 After the war

President Abraham Lincoln, who had been elected before the war broke out, hoped to make a lasting peace but he was assassinated at Ford's Theater in Washington.

2

The south had been ruined by the war and its main town, Richmond, had been burned. For years afterwards both white and black people were very poor.

3

Some southerners still regarded black people as slaves. They formed a secret society called the Ku Klux Klan. Members covered themselves in sheets and terrorized black people.

Explorers and Empire Builders

In 1750 there were still huge areas of the world where Europeans had never been. During the 19th and late 18th centuries European explorers set out to discover as much as they could about the lands and oceans of the world. Traders and settlers followed and the European countries began to set up colonies abroad which they ruled.

Captain Cook

Captain Cook led three expeditions (1768-79) to the Pacific Ocean. He visited islands such as Tahiti where he was met by war canoes.

He explored the east coast of Australia. Its strange animals fascinated the artists and scientists on the expedition.

He also sailed round the islands of New Zealand. The crew of his ship *Endeavour* landed and met the Maoris who lived there.

1 Exploring Africa

During the 19th century people began to explore and make maps of Africa. They saw wonderful sights such as the Victoria Falls, but many fell ill and died of strange diseases.

2 On a journey in search of the source of the Nile, two British explorers, Speke and Grant, stayed with Mutesa, King of Buganda, who treated them with great hospitality.

3 Some explorers, such as Dr Livingstone, were also Christian missionaries.* Missionaries set up hospitals and schools for the Africans, as well as churches.

4 The Frenchman, René Caillé, was one of the earliest European explorers in the Sahara Desert. He was also one of the first Europeans to see the ancient African city of Timbuktu.

5 There were also several women explorers in the 19th century. This is Alexandrine Tinné, a wealthy Dutch heiress, who travelled through much of North Africa and the Sudan.

*People who went to foreign lands to teach the people about Christianity.

Other expeditions

1 Richard Burton was a daring explorer. He disguised himself to visit the Arab holy city, Mecca, where only Muslims were allowed.

2 Many explorers never returned from the jungles of South America where they went to make maps and search for lost cities.

3 Later explorers travelled to the frozen north and south. In 1909, Robert Peary, an American, was the first to reach the North Pole. Roald Amundsen reached the South Pole in 1911.

Setting up colonies

1 Europeans wanted new places to sell their factory-made goods. They also wanted to buy raw materials such as cotton and tea.

2 If quarrels between local rulers threatened trade, the Europeans sent armies. These often stayed after the fighting was over.

3 They also sent officials to organize and govern the territory for them, thus setting up a colony there.

4 More and more Europeans went to the colonies and settled there with their families. They organized vast estates where the local people worked and grew tea, rubber, cotton and foodstuffs or reared sheep and cattle. Later, when minerals were discovered, factories and railways were built and still more people went to live in the colonies.

5 In Europe, politicians were worried by the increase in population and they encouraged people to go and settle in the colonies where there was land and work for them.

Europeans in Africa

1 North Africa

In the early 19th century most of the countries of North Africa were part of the Ottoman Empire*. But the Ottoman Empire was breaking up and European powers began to move in.

The French gained control of Algeria and later Tunisia and Morocco. Here, desert tribesmen are attacking one of the French forts, which is defended by the famous French Foreign Legion.

2

The ruler of Egypt needed money, so he sold his shares in the Suez Canal to Britain. Britain became involved in Egyptian affairs and later took over the government.

3

Egypt also ruled the Sudan. In 1883 a religious leader, the Mahdi, led a revolt. Britain sent an army led by General Gordon, but it was defeated at Khartoum.

Trading in the West

These gold objects were made by the Ashanti, a people who live in west Africa. They grew rich by trading in gold and slaves. They fought the British in several wars and were defeated in 1901.

Zimbabwe

Zimbabwe was the capital city of a rich kingdom in south-east Africa. It was destroyed probably in the early 19th century by rival tribes. The people were clever builders and this is the remains of a temple in the city.

*Empire of Muslim people from Middle East called the Ottoman Turks.

1 South Africa

Cecil Rhodes

Dutch settlers had first arrived in South Africa in 1652. They set up Cape Colony on the Cape of Good Hope. Most of them were farmers and they became known as "Boers" (Dutch word for farmers). In 1814 an international treaty gave Cape Colony to the British. The Boers hated being ruled by the British and between 1835 and 1837 many of them set off northwards, with all their possessions in wagons, to find new lands free from British rule. This movement is called the "Great Trek".

Cecil Rhodes made a fortune from diamond and gold mines, then formed a company to build a railway from the British colony to the mining area north of the Boer states. In 1895 this area became known as Rhodesia.

The Grab for Africa

- FRENCH
- BRITISH
- GERMAN
- PORTUGUESE
- BELGIAN
- SPANISH
- ITALIAN

In 1880 much of Africa was still independent of any European country. Between 1880 and the outbreak of World War I in 1914, the European powers carved up nearly the whole of Africa between them. This map shows Africa in 1914.

The Boers came into conflict with the Zulus, the fiercest of the neighbouring African tribes. The British helped the Boers and eventually, in 1879, the Zulus were completely defeated.

The British gradually increased their control over the Boer states. In 1886, gold was discovered in one of them and many more British people came out to work in them.

In 1899 war broke out between the Boers and the British. The Boers did very well at first. They rode fast horses, were good at stalking the enemy and knew the countryside.

The British destroyed the Boers' farms and animals and put all the Boers they could find, including women and children, into special prison camps. In 1902 the Boers surrendered.

Key dates

AD1814	Britain gained control of Cape Colony.
c. AD1830	Collapse of Kingdom of Zimbabwe.
AD1830	French began to take over North Africa.
AD1835/1837	The Great Trek.
AD1875	Britain bought Egypt's shares in the Suez Canal.
AD1878/9	Zulu War.
AD1885	Fall of Khartoum.
AD1896	Britain took over Matabeleland which became Rhodesia.
AD1899/1902	Boer War.
AD1901	Ashanti kingdom became British.
AD1910	Union of South Africa set up.

The British in India

1 This is a court of the British East India Company which started as a trading company. By the 19th century it governed most of India.

2 The British built railways and schools and tried to modernize India. They also tried to stop some of the Indians' religious customs. The Indians resented this interference. In 1857 some *sepoys* (Indian soldiers in the British Army) mutinied and the revolt quickly spread. The British eventually regained control but in future changes were made more carefully.

3 After the Mutiny the East India Company lost its right to rule and the British Government appointed its own officials. Indian princes also lost their power but were very wealthy and still lived in great luxury.

4 Queen Victoria became Empress of India in 1876. Many Indians felt this created a special tie with Britain and the royal family often went to India.

5 The British brought their own customs and entertainments to India. They introduced cricket which became one of the national sports of India.

6 Most Indians were very poor. The cities were crowded and outbreaks of disease and famines were common. Improvements could be made only slowly.

7 The two main religious groups in India were the Hindus and the Muslims. They were rivals and sometimes there were riots and people were killed.

8 The Indians had little say in how their country was ruled so a group of them formed the National Congress. At first they just wanted reforms but later they began to demand independence from Britain.

Convicts and Settlers

1 In 1788 the British Government began to send criminals to Australia as a punishment. Many stayed on there after they had served their sentence.

2 Soon many other settlers arrived. Most of them wanted land where they could raise sheep and cattle. Some went in search of gold and minerals.

3 Life in Australia in the 19th century was hard and often dangerous. There were "bushrangers" (outlaws). The most famous was Ned Kelly.

4 As more settlers arrived they took land from the Aborigines (native Australians), many of whom were killed, or died of diseases brought by settlers.

INDIA

Key dates

AD1788 First convicts sent to Australia.
AD1840 Britain claimed New Zealand.
AD1857 Indian Mutiny.
AD1876 **Queen Victoria** became Empress of India.
AD1885 Indian National Congress party founded.

BRITISH TERRITORY IN 1914

AUSTRALIA

NEW ZEALAND

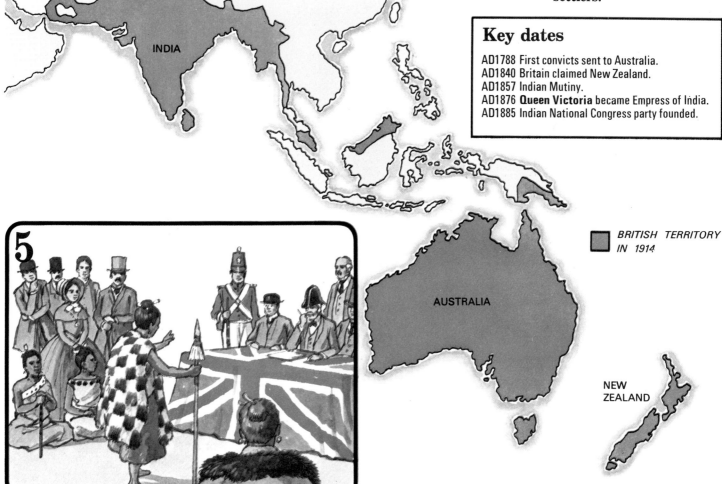

5 European settlers first arrived in New Zealand in the 1790s. In 1840 the British Government took over the country. The Governor and the Maori chiefs made a treaty agreeing how much land the settlers could have, but this did not prevent fierce wars between the Maoris and the settlers.

This map shows British territory in India, South-East Asia, and Australia in 1914. By this time Australia and New Zealand had gained the right to rule themselves but they were still part of the British Empire.

Indians and Settlers

Many tribes of Indians lived in North America, each with its own way of life and language. The Indians of the Great Plains lived by farming until they captured horses from the Spaniards in the 16th century. Then most of them became nomads, hunting buffalo across the Plains and rearing horses. They lived like this for about 200 years until European settlers moved west and took the Indians' hunting grounds for their farms.

Tepee (tent made of buffalo hide)

Buffalo hunt. The buffalo provided Indians with food, clothing and shelter.

Chiefs

Traders

Meat drying

We have removed part of this tepee wall so you can see inside.

Travois (sledge)

Medicine man

Preparing buffalo hide

The Plains Indians lived in tepees which could be packed up when the buffalo moved on. The first white men to meet the Indians were traders who sold metal goods, blankets and guns and bought buffalo hides and horses.

1 Settlers move west

As more settlers from Europe moved into the original 13 States of the United States of America, more land was needed. In 1803 the Americans bought Louisiana from the French.

Settlers began to cross the Appalachian Mountains and the Great Plains, looking for land to farm. They travelled with wagons packed with everything they needed

for their new homes, so most people, except for guards and cattle herders had to walk. It usually took many months to reach a suitable area.

2 The settlers made treaties with the Indians promising not to take all their land. But the treaties were soon broken when settlers wanted more land.

3 In 1848 gold was discovered in California. Thousands of people flocked there in the "goldrush" hoping to make fortunes.

4 Railways were built to link the east and west coasts. These brought more settlers to the Great Plains, leaving less and less land for the Indians.

5 The men who built the tracks had to be fed. They employed hunters armed with rifles who killed most of the buffalo on which the Indians had depended.

6 The Indians fought the settlers. The wars were bitter and both sides were cruel. The Indians won victories such as at Little Big Horn when they killed

General Custer and his men. But the settlers had more soldiers and better weapons and many Indian tribes were almost wiped out.

7 The Indians were left with only small areas of land called reservations. They were controlled by government agents and most were very unhappy.

The Wild West

In the United States of America, many of the people who moved westwards to the vast plains and prairies started raising cattle or growing corn. Towns, like this one, grew up to supply their needs. At first they were wild, lawless places, especially when cowboys from the ranches came into town. They brought great herds of cattle to the railway depots from which they were taken to feed the people in the cities.

Large industries and cities like New York and Chicago grew up. The first skyscrapers were built. By 1890 the United States was one of the world's most powerful industrial nations.

At first life was hard for the farmers on the plains, but soon they started using tougher crops and steel ploughs and later bought machines for harvesting and threshing. Before long they were producing vast quantities of grain which were sold all over the world.

From all over Europe poor people and people persecuted for their ideas came to the United States to start a new life. Some were lucky, but many of them ended up working in factories and living in hard conditions in the big cities.

New Countries in South America

1

Between 1810 and 1825 a series of revolutions ended the rule of Spain and Portugal in South America and set up 11 new states. This is Simon Bolivar, one of the revolutionary leaders who helped to achieve this.

2

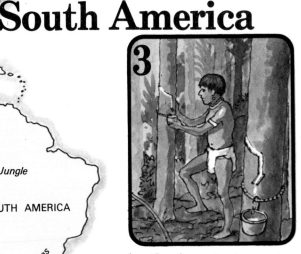

Coffee was brought from Arabia to South America and grown on large estates. By 1860 it was the main export of many states.

3

Another important export was rubber. It was made from the juice of trees growing in the Amazon jungle.

4

Many of the Indian tribes in the Amazon jungle attacked the white men who came to take over their lands.

5

On the vast pampas (grasslands) of the south-east, there were huge ranches where great herds of cattle were reared by cowboys called "gauchos".

The cattle were used for making canned meat which was sold abroad.

1 Mexico

Mexicans and Americans were always quarrelling about who should control Texas. It belonged to Mexico but many Americans had settled there and wanted to be part of the United States. Here Davy Crockett and a group of other Americans are defending the Alamo Fort against a Mexican attack.

2

In 1863 the European powers, led by France, tried to get control of Mexico by making Archduke Maximilian of Austria, Emperor of Mexico. In 1867 the Mexicans shot him.

3

From 1867 onwards the Mexicans ruled themselves. In the early 20th century civil war broke out. One of the revolutionary leaders was Pancho Villa, shown here.

Life Under the Tsars

1

The Tsars (emperors) of Russia governed their huge country from St Petersburg. There was no parliament and the Tsars and nobles, from whom they chose their ministers and officials, were very cut off from the rest of the country. Much of their time was spent at balls and receptions.

2

Most Russians were members of the Orthodox Christian Church, which supported the idea that the Tsar was chosen by God and that he alone had the right to rule.

3

Talking or writing about government reforms was forbidden. Secret police tracked down anyone suspected of wanting to change the government.

4

Many people who criticized the government for its inefficiency and cruelty, were executed or sent into exile in a part of Russia called Siberia.

5

During the 19th century there were several great novelists, playwrights and composers at work in Russia. The Russian ballet became world-famous.

6

Many Russians were serfs—peasants who lived on nobles' estates and were treated as slaves. Serfs could be bought and sold. They had to do any work their estate owner demanded and they were often given cruel punishments for small mistakes. There were frequent uprisings and riots. Eventually, in 1861, Tsar Alexander II freed the serfs. The government lent them money to buy land, but they were too poor to buy farming equipment and pay back the loans. Their lives were not much improved and some were even worse off than before.

The Crimean War

The Russians wanted to expand their empire. In the late 18th and early 19th centuries they expanded eastwards. They also won land around the Black Sea, by helping the people of these territories free themselves from the Turkish Empire. The countries of Europe were suspicious of Russia's ambitions. In 1853 Britain and France tried to capture the area called the Crimea, to stop Russian expansion. One incident in this war was the Charge of the Light Brigade (shown here). A British force misunderstood an order and charged the Russian guns.

1 Discontent grows

This is Nicholas II, who became Tsar in 1894. He was a well-meaning and kind man but he was not strong enough to be a good ruler.

2

Nicholas's wife, Alexandra, was under the spell of a monk called Rasputin. She believed he could cure her son of a blood disease, but others thought him evil.

3

Factories and industrial towns were growing up in Russia. Living conditions in the towns were very bad and many people started demanding changes.

4

In 1905 a crowd of workers went on strike and marched to the Tsar's palace to tell him their problems. Soldiers, fearing a revolution, fired on them.

5

The Tsar allowed a *Duma* (parliament) to meet for a while but then dismissed it. Meanwhile, a group of people in exile, led by Lenin, were planning a revolution.

Key dates

AD1762/1796	Reign of **Catherine the Great**.
AD1812	Invasion of Russia by Napoleon.
AD1853/1856	Crimean War.
AD1855/1881	Reign of **Alexander II**.
AD1861	Serfs freed.
AD1894/1917	Reign of **Nicholas II**.
AD1904/1905	Russia defeated in war with Japan.
AD1905	Massacre of strikers outside Tsar's palace.
AD1906	Meeting of Duma (parliament).

Western Ideas in the East

Japan

From about 1640 onwards Japan had no contact with the countries of the west, except for a few Dutch traders. Then, in 1853, Commodore Perry, the commander of a squadron of American warships, sailed to Japan and got permission for America to trade with Japan. Soon European powers followed and Japan made trade agreements with many European countries.

It was hundreds of years since any emperor of Japan had had any real power. An official called the Shogun ruled the country for the emperor. This is the last Shogun of Japan.

In 1868 the 15-year-old Emperor left the old capital, Kyoto, and set up a new one in Edo (Tokyo). Here he is arriving in Edo, where he took back power from the Shogun and set up a western-style parliament.

The small picture above shows the opening of the first parliament.

The Samurai (warriors) were replaced by a new army, trained in modern methods of fighting by advisers from France and Germany.

The Japanese learnt many other things from the west. They built railways and factories and started producing large numbers of goods quickly and cheaply.

The Japanese wanted to win power overseas. They started to interfere in China and Korea. This made them rivals with the Russians and in 1904 Japan and Russia went to war. The new, efficient Japanese army and navy quickly defeated the Russians.

1 China

Between 1644 and 1912, China was ruled by the Ch'ing (also called the Manchu) Emperors. One of the greatest was Ch'ien Lung (1736-95), shown here.

The Ch'ing emperors fought many wars to protect their frontiers, win more territory and put down rebellions. At first they were successful but the wars were very expensive and later emperors found it more and more difficult to pay for them. The country slowly became weaker.

The Chinese population was growing quickly but farming methods were still very old-fashioned. It was difficult to grow enough food for everyone.

The Chinese Government did not like foreigners and allowed them to trade only in certain areas. The British were keen to extend these areas and in 1839 they went to war.

The British won the war in 1842. They forced the Chinese to sign a treaty which gave them Hong Kong and allowed them to trade in certain other ports.

Some Chinese decided to strengthen China by adopting certain Western ideas and inventions, such as railways, and steamships. But many still hated foreign ideas.

People who hated foreigners formed a secret society called the "Boxers". In 1900 they started attacking all the foreigners they could find in China. Here they are storming a foreign embassy.

This is the Empress Tzu Hsi. From 1862 to 1908 she ruled China, first for her son, then for her nephew. She often plotted with those who hated foreigners.

In 1911 there was a revolution and the last Ch'ing Emperor was expelled from China. This is Sun Yat-sen the first President of China.

Time Chart

	North America	Central and South America	Europe	Africa
	Mound Builders living on the plains.		Gradual conversion of barbarian kingdoms to Christianity.	North Africa and Egypt part of the Byzantine Empire. North Africa and Egypt overrun by Muslim Arabs.
AD800		Decline of Maya civilization in Mexico.	Invasion of Spain by Muslims. Battle of Poitiers. Muslim advance into Western Europe halted. Viking raids begin. **Charlemagne** crowned Holy Roman Emperor.	Various tribes start living south of the Sahara Desert.
AD900				
AD1000	Vikings may have reached America.		Normans invade England. Normans invade Italy.	First Iron Age settlement at Zimbabwe.
AD1100		Chimu people living in Peru.	First Crusade.	Zimbabwe becomes a powerful kingdom.
AD1200			The Mongols invade Eastern Europe. Eighth Crusade.	Arab merchants known to be trading in West and East Africa. Rise of Empire of Mali in West Africa.
AD1300		Rise of Aztec Empire in Mexico.	Beginning of Hundred Years War. Black Death from Asia spreads through Europe.	
AD1400	People living at Huff.	Spread of Inca Empire in Peru.	First firearms developed. Invention of printing. Ideas of the Renaissance spreading from Italy.	Chinese merchants trading in East Africa. Kingdom of Benin set up. Portuguese expeditions explore
AD1500	Voyage of Christopher Columbus.	Arrival of Spaniards. End of Aztec and Inca Empires. Arrival of Portuguese.	European explorers discover America. Beginning of Reformation. Wars of Religion between Catholic and Protestants.	west coast and start trading with Africans. Turks conquered Egypt. Mali Empire destroyed. Beginning of slave trade.
AD1600	Spaniards brought horses to America. First European settlements. Pilgrim Fathers arrive in New England.		Development of trade between Europe and other parts of the world. English Civil War.	Dutch settlers arrive in South Africa.
AD1700	England wins Canada from the French. War of American Independence.		Beginning of Agricultural Revolution in Britain. Beginning of Industrial Revolution in Britain. French Revolution.	Rise of Ashanti power on west coast.
AD1800	United States buys Louisiana from the French. California goldrush. American Civil War.	Spaniards and Portuguese driven out of Central and South America. War between Mexico and United States of America.	**Wars of Napoleon** Unification of Italy. Unification of Germany.	Slave trade abolished within British Empire. The Great Trek. Opening of Suez Canal. European powers build up empires in Africa. Boer war begins. Union of South Africa
AD1900		Mexican Revolution begins.	World War I.	established.

Russia and Asia	Middle East	India	China and Japan	Far East and Pacific
Slavs in Russia. Muslims conquer Persia.	Byzantine Empire controls much of Middle East. Death of **Muhammad.** Spread of Muslim Empire. Muslims conquer much of Byzantine Empire.	India ruled by many princes.	T'ang Dynasty in China.	
			Japanese capital moved to Kyoto.	
Vikings settle in Russia. Kiev becomes most important city in Russia.				Rise of the Khmers in Cambodia. First settlers reach Easter Island and New Zealand from Polynesia.
Russia becomes offically Christian.	Seljuk Turks invade Byzantine Empire. Invasion of Seljuk Turks. The First Crusade. Kingdom of Outremer founded. Life of **Saladin.**		Sung Dynasty in China. Appearance of Samurai in Japan. Military rulers in Japan take the title "Shogun".	Large statues erected on Easter Island.
Mongols invade and conquer Russia.	Sack of Constantinople by Crusaders. End of Kingdom of Outremer.		**Marco Polo** visits China. The Mongol ruler, **Kubilai Khan,** conquers China. Ming Dynasty in China.	
		Mongols invade northern India.		
Rise of Moscow. Russia gradually united. **Ivan III** becomes first Tsar and throws off Mongol power. Rise of Safavid Dynasty in Persia. **Tsar Ivan the Terrible.** Development of trade between Russia and England. **Tsar Peter the Great.**	Sack of Constantinople by Ottoman Turks. End of Byzantine Empire. **Suleiman the Magnificent.** Turks threaten Europe. Turkish advance into Europe halted. Europeans try to extend their trade with Turkey and Persia.	First European sea voyage to India and back, led by **Vasco da Gama** (Portuguese). Mogul Empire set up. British start regular trade with India.	Long period of war in Japan. Arrival in Japan and China of European traders and missonaries. All Europeans, except Dutch traders, expelled from Japan. The Manchu family start the Ch'ing Dynasty in China.	Europeans first see Pacific Ocean. First Europeans cross Pacific Ocean on their way round the world. Expansion of Dutch trade in East Indies.
		British destroy French power in India.		Dutch land in Australia. **Captain Cook** reaches Australia and New Zealand. British colony of Australia founded.
Napoleon's expedition to Moscow. Crimean War. **Nicholas II** becomes Tsar. Meeting of the First Duma (parliament).	Ottoman Empire falling apart. Russia tries to help parts of Empire break free. World War I.	Britain gradually gains control of the whole of India. Indian Mutiny. **Queen Victoria** proclaimed Empress of India.	War between the British and Chinese. **Commodore Perry** arrives in Japan. Boxer uprising in China. War between Japan and Russia. Revolution in China. Last Ch'ing Emperor expelled.	Britain takes possession of New Zealand. French build up empire in Indo-China.

95

Index

Going Further

Books to read

These are just some of the books available on these periods of history. If you look in your local library or book shop, you will probably find many others.

AD600 to AD1450

The Time Traveller Book of Viking Raiders by Anne Civardi and James Graham-Campbell (Usborne).
The Time Traveller Book of Knights and Castles by Judy Hindley (Usborne).
Castle by David Macaulay (Collins).
Living in a Medieval Village, Living in a Medieval City and *Living in a Crusader Land*—3 books by R. J. Unstead (Black).
Knight Crusader by Ronald Welch (Puffin).
The Children's Crusade by Henry Treece (Puffin).
Vinland the Good by Henry Treece (Puffin).
The Buildings of Early Islam by Helen and Richard Leacroft (Hodder and Stoughton).
The Samurai of Japan and *Genghis Khan and the Mongols*—2 books by Michael Gibson (Wayland).
Peoples of the Past, The Aztecs by Judith Crosher (Macdonald).

AD1450 to AD1750

Everyday Life in Renaissance Times by E. R. Chamberlin (Carousel).
The Story of Britain in Tudor and Stuart Times by R. J. Unstead (Carousel).

Europe Finds the World, The Birth of Modern Europe, Martin Luther and *Benin*—4 books in the Cambridge Introduction to the History of Mankind (Cambridge University Press).
Cue for Treason by Geoffrey Trease (Puffin).
Popinjay Stairs by Geoffrey Trease (Puffin).
The Strangers by Anne Schlee (Puffin).
Jack Holborn by Leon Garfield (Puffin).

AD1750 to AD1914

The Old Regime and the Revolution, Power for the People, The War of American Independence and *Transported to Van Diemen's Land*—4 books in the Cambridge Introduction to the History of Mankind (Cambridge University Press).
Honest Rogues: The Inside Story of Smuggling by Harry T. Sutton (Batsford-Heritage).
Freedom and Revolution and *Age of Machines* by R. J. Unstead (Macdonald).
Ishi: Last of his Tribe by Theodore Kroeber (Puffin).
Underground to Canada by Barbara C. Smucker (Puffin).
Children on the Oregon Trail by A. Rutgers Van Der Loeff (Puffin).
Escape from France by Ronald Welch (Puffin).
Castors Away! by Hester Burton (Puffin).
*These books are novels.

Places to visit

There are lots of places where you can see things from these periods of history. Most museums have furniture, costumes, weapons and everyday objects in their collections. If you live in Britain, two books that will help you find out about places to visit in your area are *Museums and Galleries in Great Britain and Ireland* (ABC Publications) and *Historic Houses, Castles and Gardens in Great Britain and Ireland* (ABC Publications), which you can buy in newsagents and book shops. Both these books are published every year.

Paintings can tell you a lot too, They often show the clothes and houses of the people who had them painted. Look in art galleries and at art books in libraries. Photographs can tell you a lot about the latter part of the period.

Look out for great houses and houses once lived in by famous people. Look out too for factories and farms built after 1750. *History Around Us* by Nathaniel Harris (Hamlyn) and *History Hunter* by Victor E. Neuburg (Beaver Books) will help you to recognize them.

In London the British Museum, The Victoria and Albert Museum and the London Museum all have collections of things from these periods of history.

In Australia the National Gallery of Victoria in Melbourne has a good collection of objects from Cambodia, China and Japan. It is also worth visiting the museums in Perth and Sydney.

In Canada the best museums to visit are the Royal Ontario Museum in Toronto and the McCord Museum in Montreal.